On Pascha

With the Fragments of Melito and Other Material Related to the Quartodecimans

MELITO OF SARDIS

Translated, introduced, and annotated by

ALISTAIR STEWART-SYKES

ST VLADIMIR'S SEMINARY PRESS
CRESTWOOD, NEW YORK

Library of Congress Cataloging-in-Publication Data

Melito, Saint, Bishop of Sardis, 2nd cent.
    [Homily on the passion. English]
    On Pascha: with the fragments of Melito and other material related to the
quartodecimans / Melito of Sardis; translated, introduced and annotated by
Alistair Stewart-Sykes
        p.   cm.
    Includes bibliographical references and index.
    ISBN 0–88141–217–1 (alk. paper)
    ISBN 978–0-88141–217–8
    ISSN 1555–5755
    1. Jesus Christ—Passion—Sermons—Early works to 1800.   2. Sermons,
Greek—Early works to 1800.   3. Sermons, English—Early works to 1800.
I. Stewart-Sykes, Alistair.   II. Title.

BR65.M453 H6513 2001
252'.63—dc21

                                                                00–051815

ISBN 0–88141–217–1
ISBN 978–0–88141–217–8
ISSN 1555–5755

Contents

For Alice
with love

PREFACE

This work is not a scientific translation of *On Pascha,* but a fairly free rendition intended for students, seminarians, working clergy and faithful Christians. I would hope that this audience would get an idea of the contents and style of *On Pascha*, and some indication of its significance, particularly with regard to our understanding of the earliest paschal liturgy. In translating I have had a view to the rhetorical quality of the text, and in particular to the fact that the piece was designed to be spoken aloud, and scientific accuracy was therefore prized less highly than euphony.

The text employed is that of Hall, who also provides an excellent translation; my debt to Hall's work will be manifest on every page and those requiring an apparatus and accuracy at every point should turn to Hall, rather than to the present work. The reader will also find frequent reference to my work *The Lamb's High Feast*, published two years ago; I have taken the opportunity here to correct some of the less guarded statements found in that work, particularly with regard to Hippolytus, and to expand on a few points, particularly with regard to Melito's *eunouchia* (as a result of a conversation with colleagues in a tea-shop!)

The class on "The Jewish roots of Christian liturgy," taught at the General Seminary in New York in 2000, was subjected to some of this material, and even managed to make some contributions to the effort. The manuscript was proofread by Gloria Bowden of the Diocese of Atlanta, and the editor of this series, Dr John Behr, showed diligence and patience in equal measure in preparing it for the press.

I have been studying Melito since 1987, assisted by his prayers and those of all the saints, and continue to find new depths in his work. I hope that through this work my audience will be able to share something of this pleasure. In time I hope that the dedicatee will be part of the audience.

Alistair Stewart-Sykes
New York
On the feast of Saint Alban,
protomartyr of Britain, 2000

INTRODUCTION

Melito

Late in the second century, Victor, then leading bishop in Rome, sought to gain some unity in the manner in which the mystery of the Lord's death and resurrection was celebrated in Rome. Rome was not a united church at the time but a loose federation of churches, and immigrant groups tended to keep their ancestral customs. Asian Christians in particular kept a festival on the fourteenth day of the Jewish month of Nisan, at the same time as the Jewish Passover, at which they commemorated the death and resurrection of the Lord. In time they became known as Quartodecimans, since they kept the fourteenth day, but this usage, deriving from the Latin *quarta decima*, which means "fourteenth" is later.

It is hard to determine all the details of Victor's involvement in the Quartodeciman controversy, but somehow the Asian bishops were drawn into the dispute. Eusebius writes of Victor as a monarch bishop claiming a rather wider jurisdiction than he actually held, summoning synods in the various Asian cities.[1] It is more likely that Asian communities in Rome, whose customs were being questioned by Victor, the leading elder among the churches, looked to their ancestral homeland for support and assistance. One of the traditional duties of the leading presbyter-bishop in Rome was correspondence with other churches, which is the capacity in which

---

1 Eusebius *Ecclesiastical History*, 5.23; this document may be found below on pp. 84-85.

Clement writes to the Corinthians in the letter known as *I Clement*, and so as "foreign secretary" Victor, once the Asian bishops had been drawn in, would have become even further involved, and his further involvement would increase Eusebius' impression that Victor was "Pope". Whatever the manner in which he became involved, a letter from Polycrates, bishop of Ephesus, to Victor is recorded by Eusebius, in which are mentioned notable figures who had kept Pascha on the fourteenth of Nisan. Among them is mentioned "Melito the eunuch who governed entirely in the Holy Spirit, who lies at Sardis..."[2]

We may deduce a number of significant points about Melito from the letter of Polycrates. Firstly we may deduce that Melito was a Quartodeciman, that he kept Pascha on the fourteenth of Nisan in accordance with the custom that had been handed down from Judaism.[3] Secondly we may note that, compared to the other authorities whom Polycrates cites such as Philip and John the apostles, Melito had but recently died at the time in which Polycrates wrote. If this is the case we may date his death to ca 190. Hall dates Melito's *Apology* fairly precisely between 169 and 177, and, on the basis of a notice in Eusebius with which we shall deal below, he dates *On Pascha* uncontroversially, though by no means certainly, between 160 and 170.[4] We may accept his dating for the *Apology*, but shall

---

2   Quoted by Eusebius at *Ecclesiastical History,* 5.24; this letter may be
    found below on pp. 86-87.
3   Although some voices have been raised doubting that Melito was indeed
    a Quartodeciman, or that the work here attributed to Melito of Sardis is
    the work of a different author altogether this need not detain the reader of
    this introduction. For details and bibliography see A. Stewart-Sykes *The
    Lamb's High Feast: Melito, Peri Pascha and the Quartodeciman paschal
    liturgy at Sardis* (Leiden: Brill, 1998), 2-3, 6-7.
4   S.G. Hall, ed. and trans., *Melito of Sardis: On Pascha and Fragments*
    (Oxford: Clarendon, 1979), xii with reference to Eusebius, *Ecclesiastical History,* 4.26.1.

suggest that the notice in Eusebius is of little help in dating *On Pascha*. Nonetheless we may gather from the dating of the *Apology* and from Melito's position in Polycrates' catalogue that Melito flourished in the third quarter of the second century.

Thirdly we may deduce from Polycrates' statements here that Melito was Jewish by birth. Polycrates lists seven great lights of Asia who had been Quartodecimans, and then adds himself as a "supernumerary eighth." The particular great lights enumerated by Polycrates have been chosen for some reason and Bauckham suggests that they are named because Polycrates is claiming that he is himself related to all of these in some way. Polycrates indeed states that those mentioned are all his relatives (*suggeneis*).[5] But this of itself does not explain why Polycrates should wish to point out his network of relationships. Normal classical usage employs the term *suggenês* ("relative") and its cognates to mean relationships within an extended family or within a nation, and to refer to relationships between families claiming a connection or states claiming a common origin, and actually excludes close blood relationship. This is the probable sense in which Polycrates employs the term. The only possible set of relationships to which Polycrates may be referring is Jewish; Paul uses the same term to refer to fellow-Jews when he speaks in Romans of his relatives according to the flesh.[6] Polycrates' argument is then not only that seven great Asian lights, including the apostle John, were Quartodeciman, but by implication that this is an ancient practice derived from Judaism. Melito was Jewish by birth, an attribute which he shares with a number of significant leaders of the Asian Christians.

5 Richard Bauckham "Papias and Polycrates on the origin of the Fourth Gospel," *Journal of Theological Studies*, ns 44 (1993), 24-69 at 29-30.
6 Romans 9:3.

Fourthly we may deduce from Polycrates' writing that Melito was Bishop of Sardis. Hall notes that whereas Polycrates names some as bishops, Melito is not given this distinction, and suggests that the identification of Melito as bishop is the work of Eusebius.[7] He is able to note in this context that Ignatius of Antioch writes no letter to the Church at Sardis. The two reasons given for Ignatius' failure to write a letter to the church in Sardis are that there was no bishop, or that the extent of Judaistic practice at Sardis made Ignatius inimical to this Christian community. The second reason is the more probable given the extensive ties, including Quartodeciman practice, between the Christianity of Sardis and its Jewish roots; but even if the first explanation is the correct one, and there was no bishop at the time of Ignatius, this is hardly relevant for the time of Melito, perhaps some fifty years later. We may agree with Hall that Eusebius' description of Melito as bishop is certainly beside the point; however those described as bishops in Polycrates' list are also martyrs, and it may be this double qualification that causes him to employ the term at this point. But Polycrates does state, elsewhere in his letter, that Melito was bishop. After his mention of the seven great lights of Asia (the last of whom is Melito) who kept the fourteenth, Polycrates goes on to say: "seven of my relatives were bishops." These are the seven who kept the fourteenth day, and who were fellow Jews with Polycrates. Melito is among them, as bishop. Moreover, Polycrates refers to Melito "governing all things in the Holy Spirit." Lawlor and Oulton translate this phrase as "lived in the Holy Spirit" and take it as a reference to Melito's piety.[8] Although "living" is a possible

7   Hall, *Melito of Sardis: On Pascha,* xii.
8   H.J. Lawlor and J.E.L. Oulton, *Eusebius: The Ecclesiastical History and the Martyrs of Palestine* II (London: SPCK, 1928), 186-7.

translation of the Greek verb *politeuomai*, we would not expect an object (*panta*); the word is however used with an object by classical authors to refer to systems of government, or to the act of governing, and on this basis we may suggest that Polycrates is speaking of Melito's governance of the church in the Holy Spirit.

Finally, we must deal with Polycrates' puzzling description of Melito as "the eunuch". Early in her treatment of the parallel prosopographies of Favorinus and Polemo, the former of whom was a eunuch, Maud Gleason writes:

> Congenital eunuchs are a rare phenomenon and eunuchs of any sort were probably not a daily sight in the provincial cities of the western empire at this time, or even in the east, where self-castrated priests were traditionally associated with certain religious cults (Lucian *De Dea Syria*, 51-52). Castrated slaves were not as commonly seen as they were in later centuries, although grisly how-to instructions were available in medical texts. We may assume that at this time eunuchs with social position were practically unknown.[9]

In taking this statement as a starting point for our examination of Melito's *eunouchia* a few refinements may be made. Although there was a traditional association between the cult of Cybele and self-castration the evidence for such an association in the second century is thin, as it rests entirely on one work of Lucian which is written in a strange Herodotean style. Lucian's *De Dea Syria* is a traveler's tale, a self-conscious work of fiction which provides no evidence of value for the period of its writing. Secondly, although castrated slaves were perhaps not a daily sight, ample evidence of castrated slaves in the

---

9 Maud W. Gleason, *Making Men: Sophists and Self-presentation in Ancient Rome* (Princeton: Princeton UP, 1995), 6.

second century is provided by Guyot, including a significant number in Asia.[10] However it is fair to say that eunuchs with social position were practically unknown. Interestingly the only roughly contemporary congenital eunuch of status she is able to find is Dorotheus, a Christian presbyter at Antioch.[11]

Melito's *eunouchia* has resulted in the suggestion that he was a converted priest of Cybele. But given that the only evidence for such a practice at the time of Melito is that provided by Lucian, this may be safely discounted. Moreover the manner in which the term is attached to Melito's name would indicate that a trope is in play rather than a physical description. In line with the recognition of the term as a trope, the general interpretation offered is that it means that Melito was celibate. It is a trope however which, given the rhetorical sophistication of Polycrates' writing, may carry more meaning than a first sight might indicate. Quintilian advises a sparing use of metaphor, the function of which is to put things before the eye of the audience in a forceful way.[12] We should thus wonder why Polycrates wishes Victor to know that Melito was celibate, why Melito's *eunouchia* should be put before Victor's eyes in this forceful way, and enquire into the wider net of meaning which the term might have in this context. If Melito, alongside the others, is standing as witness, Polycrates is briefly establishing his credibility, again in keeping with Quintilian's advice. But how, in this case, does *eunouchia* give credibility?

One clue to unpacking the trope may lie in the absence of

10 P.Guyot, *Eunuchen als Sklaven und Freigelassene in der griechisch-Römischen Antike* (Stuttgarter Beiträge zur Geschichte und Politik 14; Stuttgart, 1980).
11 Dorotheus, mentioned at Eusebius, *Ecclesiastical History*, 7.32.2, cited by Gleason, *Making Men*, 6, n23.
12 *Institutio Oratoria*, 8.6.19

social status to which Gleason points; for eunuchs in the second century were slaves. This perhaps is the reason why, although celibacy is not unknown in the ancient world outside Christianity, the term *eunouchia* is not used by non-Christian writers, but is employed by Clement and Athenagoras as the male equivalent of virginity. It is possible that *Matthew* 19:12 lies behind this usage,[13] but Christians who adopt this term, among whom must be counted the author of the first Gospel, are doing more than stating their celibacy, they are deliberately adopting a tone and name indicative of a servile status, indicating something of the manner in which they rejoice in being despised by the world and are absolutely subject to God.

Melito may have been known as the eunuch, but he is a person of high education; and we have seen that he was bishop. Although a eunuch, Melito nonetheless governs the church: indeed it is as a eunuch that he governs. He has status not only within the church but without, for given that he is bishop of his church the probability is that he is also a householder, but his real social status is being rhetorically inverted. The servile status is that which the bishop holds towards the God whom he serves, the householder plays the role of eunuch within his own household, which is the household of God. The eunuch is a servant. But a eunuch, whilst naturally a servant, is a servant of a particular kind. To illustrate the particular role of servile eunuchs we may note the significant role played by eunuchs in the *Cyropaedia* of Xenophon. Here they are servants with particular advantages to their master. Because they are cut off

---

13 Note the discussion of W. Bauer, "Mt 19:12 und die alten Christen," *Neutestamentliche Studien Georg Heinrici zu seinem 70 Geburtstag dargebracht* (Leipzig: Hinrichs, 1914), 235-244, at 236. Bauer cites Athenagoras *Supplicatio* 33.34, Clement *Stromateis* 3.1.1; 3.1.4, 3.1.91 and *Paedogogus* 3.4.26 as well as ps-Cyprian *De Sing. Cler.* 31.37 and is unsure whether Matthew plays a role in this usage or not.

from normal family life they are the perfect servants and managers, as bodyguards they show a greater bravery than any other because they have nobody they love more than their master and as objects of contempt they have an even greater loyalty to their master who honors them nonetheless. They are without familial ties, and so their master and their service is their family.[14] This is the role which Melito plays in his own church, which is not his own but that of God. But Melito the eunuch is not only a socially inverted yet perfect servant of God however, for yet more lies behind the statement of Polycrates than that Melito was the ideal bishop due to his commitment in service. The point is the absence of familial ties which Melito professed. Ascetically practiced celibacy is part of this but does not exhaust the meaning, for *eunouchia* took one out of family networks altogether. We have already seen that Melito's embrace of Christ alienated him from his Jewish family. Melito as Jew had cut himself off from his family as a result of his embrace of Christianity and stands as an exemplar of one whose alienation from his own race is complete. As a man of education whose whole service is to the despised church he stands as an object of contempt, and yet he is acknowledged by Polycrates as one whose governance of the household of the church was perfect in the Spirit. Celibacy may have been part of this, but not as an end in itself but as a means by which he could be a yet more perfect servant to his master. Melito as eunuch represents loyalty and devotion displaced from the more usual network of family-relationships to the church, and more particularly to its Lord.

14 See especially Xenophon, *Cyropaedia,* 7.5.59-65 and the discussion of eunuchs in Xenophon's works of Yun Lee Too "Xenophon's Cyropaedia: Disfiguring the pedagogical state," in Yun Lee Too and Niall Livingstone (eds.), *Pedagogy and Power: Rhetorics of Classical Learning* (Cambridge: CUP, 1998), 282-302.

Elsewhere Eusebius gives a list of Melito's works and quotes from his *Apology* to the Emperor Marcus Aurelius and from his *Extracts* from the Old Testament, in which Melito gives us his Old Testament canon and tells of a visit to Palestine.[15] Apart from these reports there are but a few inconclusive references in other ancient writers, which themselves are chiefly gathered from hints left by Eusebius. We must however deal with a puzzling report concerning *On Pascha* which Eusebius preserves for us: Eusebius purports to quote from *On Pascha*, but then gives us an introduction which is not only absent from the work which we possess, but appears to point to a different work altogether. Further confusion is caused because Eusebius elsewhere states that Melito wrote "two books on the Pascha." In preparation for studying this report we should note how the document translated and presented here was discovered, and the text established.

On Pascha

On Pascha was first published in 1940. This edition was based on a single, fifth century, codex, which the editor, Bonner, had assembled from two separate collections.[16] Since the colophon was missing, the work was identified as that of Melito on the basis of the heading MELEITÔN, on the grounds that its style fulfilled what might have been expected of Melito's work, and because of its conformity with Syriac fragments already in existence.[17] Bonner entitled it *On the Passion* on the basis of a fragment of Anastasius of Sinai.[18] In the following years further

---

15 Fragment 3 below, from Eusebius, *Ecclesiastical History,* 4.26.
16 Campbell Bonner, *The Homily on the Passion by Melito Bishop of Sardis and Some Fragments of the Apocryphal Ezekiel* (London: Christophers, 1940), 5-8.
17 Bonner, *Homily,* 7.
18 Fragment 7 below.

fragments and a Latin epitome were found, but the most significant discovery was that of a further, almost complete Greek
version in Papyrus Bodmer 13.[19] This was entitled *Of Melito,
On Pascha*, which suggested that the work was related to the
Quartodeciman paschal celebrations. Finally a Coptic text was
published in 1990.[20]

Although Bonner's identification of the work he had assembled as that of Melito has received widespread acceptance,
there have been a few dissenting voices. The cause of this dis-
sent derives from the report of Melito's work found in
Eusebius. This report has been subject to much debate.[21]

> In his work "Concerning the Pascha" he indicates the time
> at which he drew it up at the beginning, stating thus: When
> Servillius Paulus was proconsul of Asia, and Sagaris was
> martyred at a fitting time, there was a great dispute in
> Laodicea concerning the Pascha, which fell most fittingly
> in those days. And these things were written:

> Clement the Alexandrian records this matter in his own
> work concerning the Pascha which he says he composed
> because of Melito's writing.

Although it is possible that this is a citation from a different work
by Melito altogether, since Eusebius records elsewhere that
Melito wrote two works on the Pascha, this is not a necessary
conclusion. The account of two works might well be the result of
another work becoming attached to Melito's *On Pascha*.
Eusebius is probably working from a library catalogue and had
no direct knowledge of these works. The same is true of the

---

19 Edited by M. Testuz, *Papyrus Bodmer XIII, Méliton de Sardes Homélie
   sur la Pâque* (Geneva: Bodmer, 1960).
20 It may be found in James E. Goehring, *The Crosby Schøyen Codex: MS
   193 in the Schøyen Collection* (Louvain: Peeters, 1990).
21 Fragment 4 below, from Eusebius' *Ecclesiastical History*, 4.26.

apparent citation from Melito, the chronological note which is reproduced here. The fact that it ends with the words "these things were written" is indicative that what had gone before was not part of the work at all but a chronological note which had been appended to *On Pascha*. Finally the fact that Clement wrote in response to Melito does not mean that Melito's work was polemical in intent, as might be deduced from the connection with the dispute at Laodicea, even were it possible with certainty to determine what was at issue in the dispute.

The most probable cause of the dispute is the time of day at which to keep the Pascha. It would seem that some Quartodecimans kept the Pascha in the early evening, at the same time as the Jews, whereas others, among whom Melito is probably to be included, postponed the celebration until the time at which the Jewish festivities ended.[22] Both practices were probably ancient, but in time problems were caused because of the difficulty of keeping the Pascha openly in the evening. Because it would be in breach of Roman law it might be seen as inviting martyrdom. A defense on the basis that Jesus kept the Pascha in this manner could be answered with reference to Melito's theory of typology according to which the lamb of the paschal meal was superseded by Christ the true paschal lamb, and that the Jewish festivity likewise was superseded and not to be kept. If Melito's work was in any way connected with this dispute it was probably a secondary involvement of this nature.

The dispute at Laodicea is impossible to date on the basis of the reference to Servillius Paulus, since no such figure is known. There are gaps in our knowledge of the proconsular years, and so it is not impossible that there was such a figure, and since the Paulli were major landowners in Asia it is also

---

22 So Stewart-Sykes, *Lamb's High Feast,* 155-160,167-172.

possible that a member of the family held another, local, office which has been confused with the proconsulate. For this reason, and because the connection with Melito's work is secondary, this chronological note is of no assistance in dating *On Pascha*. More significantly it throws no doubt on the fact that the work which has survived is that of Melito the eunuch who lies at Sardis.

The text used as the basis of this translation is that of Hall, for although the Coptic text had not been published, Hall had had access to the manuscript. Questions of text are not raised here at all, but should be followed through in Hall's critical edition.

Sardis [23]

Sardis was already an ancient city at the time of Melito. It was strategically situated on what had formerly been the great east-west highway through Asia Minor. At the time of Melito, however, it had been part of the wider Hellenistic worlds for hundreds of years, and its significance was fundamentally cultural, as a center of Hellenistic civilization standing alongside the other major cities of Asia. By the time of Melito all trace of the ancient city would have perished as the result of a major earthquake early in the first century. The city was rebuilt, largely from imperial funds. The main Roman street of the city was of marble, running along the east-west axis. It had an elevated pavement and a colonnade of shops on either side. Behind this main street to the north was the gymnasium complex, which was eventually to consist of a pair of halls one hundred meters long with an oiling room. At the time of Melito however only the gymnasium proper stood, having been finished about 166 AD. Between the gymnasium and the main street

23 For sources of all below see the suggestions for further reading.

was a thriving bazaar area, including a Jewish section. This center was situated near the Pacteolus, on the east bank, and to the north of the city, while settlement extended to the south and east, up the hillside and away from the valley itself.

Apart from its cultural significance and the presence of Melito, Sardis is of interest to students of early Christianity because it is one of the churches addressed by the seer of Revelation, and because it is also a center of Jewish civilization in Asia. In particular a vast synagogue has been unearthed at Sardis, certainly the largest and perhaps the richest Roman synagogue to have been discovered. Melito exhibits a great deal of anti-Jewish sentiment and it has often been suggested that this is the result of the differing social situation of the Christians and the Jews. This may be so, but the synagogue cannot be used to support such a claim, as it certainly was not built as a synagogue but as a public building, and was taken over for use as a synagogue only in the fourth century.

Judaism and Christianity were not the only religions at Sardis in the period. Among other religions most notable is the cult of Artemis, the civic cult. To her was dedicated the large Hellenistic temple by the Pacteolus. She appears to have taken on some of the appurtenances of the native Cybele. The worship of Sabazios was also common in Sardis but he appears to have been identified with Zeus and also with the god of the Jews; apart from Sabazios the numismatic evidence indicates that Herakles and Dionysius were also worshiped. Also significant was the imperial cultus; Sardis competed with ten other Asian cities to be the home of a temple to Tiberius, and pleaded its case before the Senate. The evidence of visits from both Marcus Aurelius and Verus, who for a time was co-Emperor with Marcus Aurelius, is an indication that imperial loyalty continued to run high in the time of Melito.

Melito the sophist

In the second century, rhetoric, an ancient skill essential for
politicians and lawyers, had grown out of these narrow con-
fines and become something akin to a spectator sport. Aristotle had defined rhetoric as being either dicanic, related to
the law court, political or persuasive, or epideictic, a branch
of oratory meant to confirm an audience in opinions which it
already held.[24] These modes of rhetoric were all practiced as
part of the education of a wealthy man in the ancient world,
and the practice of the schools, especially in epideictic oratory, which lent itself readily to display, had become more
widespread. Orators could become wealthy and enjoy great
popular success. At the same time a particular style of oratory
had developed which was known as the Asianist style. As opposed to the Attic style, which sought to use only the vocabulary and forms of the classic Athenian orators, the Asianist
style tended to be flowery, almost poetic, and innovative in
its vocabulary. Melito's rhetoric is clearly that of the Asianist
school, and we may deduce that he had received a rhetorical
education. On this basis we have sought to observe a number
of classical parallels in *On Pascha*. His adoption of rhetoric
was only natural when he came to speak of the Pascha for it
was common for religious festivals to be the occasion of rhetoric and hymnic prose.

We may note a number of rhetorical devices in Melito's
work. It is impossible to render them all in translation, but opportunity has been taken to reproduce something of Melito's
style. Among rhetorical devices we may note:

> *Homoioteleuton* (lines ending in the same way): see *On
> Pascha*, 93

24 Aristotle, *Rhetorica*, 1.3-1.9.

Homoiarcton (a series of lines beginning in the same way):
see *On Pascha,* 73

Paronomasia in antithesis (wordplay intended to point up
a contrast): the translator has contrived to create an example at *On Pascha,* 53, though this is not in the original.

Address to persons and objects not present: See the address
to the angel at *On Pascha,* 32

Asyndeton (lists not joined together with conjunctions): see
the vice list at *On Pascha,* 50

Observing Melito's rhetoric, however, goes beyond notic-
ing individual elements in the speech, because a knowledge of
the rhetorical canons of his age enables us to interpret the work
as a whole. In the first instance we should note not only that
there is great similarity in the forms of speech employed by
Melito and those used by contemporary orators, but we should
also note that rhetoric was bound up closely to religions func-
tions in the Roman Empire. The speeches which preserve for us
the most ornate style, including strings of special attributes like
that which we can see at *On Pascha* 82, are prose hymns composed on various occasions in honor of the Gods of the Empire.
Polemo, perhaps the most famous and successful orator of
Melito's time, famously dedicated the Temple of Olympian
Zeus in the presence of the Emperor Hadrian through a hymn,
composed as a speech, and delivered, he claimed, under divine
inspiration.[25] We may therefore, in view of the style of *On Pascha,* determine that Melito is presenting us not with a sermon, as
is widely held by protestant commentators, but with a liturgical
text, a speech which accompanies and effects a liturgical event.
Thus observations of similarities between Jewish hymns and

25 Philostratus, *Lives of the Sophists,* 1.533.

Byzantine Holy Week hymns,[26] even if they do not prove a
shared history or direct independence, do show that the setting
and context are the same.

In addition to seeing the context in which *On Pascha* might
be delivered, the study of rhetoric allows us to see how the
prose-hymn might fit into the liturgical action of the
Quartodecimans. Every speech had the same basic shape.
There might be other elements, and the elements might vary in
significance according to the occasion of the speech, but nonetheless the same basic template can be laid out.

Propositio/thesis: Here the orator sets out in brief what the
speech will achieve.

Narratio/diêgêma: Here the orator tells a story. In the case
of a courtroom speech it might be the facts of the case, or
else the background to the occasion. On a religious occasion a story relating to the god being praised, or to the feast,
might be told.

Probatio/kataskeuê: Here the case is proved. The *diêgêma* is
shown to be true (or false!). In a courtroom speech the weight
might well be found in this part of the speech.

Peroratio/epilogos: Here the orator sums up, ensuring the
audience is on his side, and bringing about in the audience
an emotional response proper to the occasion.

On Pascha follows this outline. Melito himself points out
the transitions from *propositio* to *narratio* and from *narratio* to
probatio, and these divisions are moreover marked off by dox-
ologies. This observation allows us to recognize the transition

26 Note, in addition to those cited in the bibliography, Panagiotos Chrestos,
   "τὸ ἐργον τοῦ Μελίτωνος Περὶ Πάσχα καὶ ἀκολουθία τοῦ πάθους"
   Kleronomia, 1 (1969), 65-78.

from *probatio* to *peroratio*, since here also there is a doxology. In the first part of the speech he sets out the fundamental themes of the Pascha, the slaughter of the sheep and the life of the Lord. In the second part he retells the story of the Egyptian passover, at first staying quite close to the scriptural text and then going on to a graphic description of the slaughter of the firstborn intended, as Greek writers on oratory suggested, to bring home an emotional response in his audience as he presents the picture. His *probatio* then sets the story in a wider perspective, that of the fall of Adam and the redemption wrought by Christ. Finally in conclusion he brings the blame on Israel, and demonstrates nonetheless the triumph of Christ. It should be noted however that in this section the guilt of Israel is played out as a counterpoint to the praise of the acts of God in redemption both under the new and the old covenants. The end of the speech finds the risen Christ present in the person and the voice of Melito, inviting the gentiles to forgiveness and to salvation.

The exceptional element to this pattern is the discussion of typology which occurs after the *narratio*. However, ancient rhetoricians were often prone to digress, and handbooks advise such a procedure. The intention was to maintain the interest of the audience by digressing in such a way that the overall interest of the speech is served. Melito does this by reflecting on the manner in which the Pascha is the fulfillment of prophecy and at the same time the fulfillment in the Lord's Pascha is the annulment of the former rite.

The pattern of *On Pascha* is thus the normal pattern of a speech. But Melito has bound this pattern to the liturgical action of the Quartodeciman Pascha, as we may see after a brief review of the paschal liturgy as Melito would have known it.

The Quartodeciman liturgy and Melito's *On Pascha*[27]

The Quartodeciman Pascha comprised what we would know both as Good Friday and as Easter, for in keeping with the Johannine tradition according to which the crucifixion was itself the manifestation of God's glory, and in keeping with the Jewish liturgical tradition of a single celebration of the Passover, the Pascha was a single festival which commemorated both the passion and the resurrection. Thus at the end of *On Pascha,* even as the events of the crucifixion are being described in counterpoint to the celebrations of the Jews, the risen Lord appears and announces his triumph.

The Quartodeciman paschal liturgy can be reconstructed as follows:

The Fast

Given that the Jewish tradition had been to keep a fast before the Passover, it is only natural that Quartodecimans should continue this tradition. Jews fasted from the time of the evening sacrifice, and the probability is that this was the original Quartodeciman practice. As the two religions parted, the original justification was forgotten. Three reasons are variously given for fasting practice:

To share in the sufferings of the Lord
To fast on behalf of the Jews during their feasting
To prepare oneself to receive Communion at the paschal feast

All of these are probably secondary, and need not be mutually exclusive. Melito contrasts the sufferings of the Lord with the celebrations of the Jews, and this is certainly an indication that he is fasting at the time the Jews are keeping their celebration.

27 For detail on all that follows below and for bibliography see *The Lamb's High Feast,* 142-206.

This celebration concluded at midnight, so it is reasonable to deduce that this was the time at which the Quartodecimans began their celebration, but that they gathered at the time at which they would once have gathered for Passover, namely around sundown on the 14th Nisan. The rationale for his fasting is probably the first, though there is also some possibility that this melds in with the second justification. This does not help us determine the point at which the fast began. Irenaeus says that there is a variety of times for which the fast is kept, and beyond this we probably cannot go. Much greater problems were caused by variation in the time at which the fast concluded: it appears that some Quartodecimans concluded the fast and began their celebration at the onset of night, the time at which the Jews likewise began their celebration, at which time other Quartodecimans would be fasting, and perhaps gathering to keep a vigil. It seems most probable, from the manner in which Melito contrasts the sufferings of the Lord with the celebrations of the Jews, that he kept a vigil for the first part of the night and that the celebration began around midnight.

The Vigil

All that can be known for certain about the vigil of the Quartodecimans is that Exodus 12 was read, as Melito tells us, and that some discussion and exposition of that reading, as found in *On Pascha*, followed. On this basis we may see the first part of *On Pascha* as the material employed by Melito in keeping this part of the vigil. We may also suggest that there was a strong eschatological tone to the night of waiting, in that just as Jews looked forward to the coming of the Messiah on the Passover night, so Christians likewise not only perceived that the Messiah came to them in the celebration and commemoration of the Pascha but believed that this might be the occasion of the Lord's final return. In a later period there is some indication that the parable of the wise and foolish virgins was read and expounded, which is further indication of the eschatological tone of the vigil. Finally there is a strong possibility that there were readings from the Old Testament prophets. This was certainly the case in Syria, as can be seen from the vigil described in the *Didascalia* which clearly derived from the same roots as that known to Melito.[28] The reading of prophecies from the Old Testament would accord with the eschatological tone of the vigil and fit in with Melito's numerous citations from the prophets.

The Celebration

Around midnight the fast was broken and the celebration, including the commemoration of the triumph of Christ amid his sufferings, would begin. *On Pascha* commemorates precisely this, and we may see that this would have accompanied the table rite as a haggadah, or declaration of God's mighty works, which Christians had inherited from Judaism, just as they inherited the custom of a joyous meal. The meal itself would have had the following shape:

I   Hors d'oevres
    First Cup of wine
II Main course (bread served at this point)
    Second cup of wine
    Meal
    Third Cup of wine

This was the shape of any formal meal in the ancient world, with the omission of a dessert. This was replaced by the final piece of bread known as the *aphikoman*, a piece broken off from the main loaf at the beginning of the meal and hidden only to be re-introduced at the conclusion of the meal. The probability is

28 *Didascalia,* 21. See the selection from this chapter at pp. 92-94 below.

that this was originally intended to represent the presence of the Messiah. Melito uses the word *aphikomenos* (coming one) suddenly at the beginning of the fourth part of *On Pascha*, and we may therefore deduce that this is the moment at which the meal concluded, after the hearing of the basic haggadah which constitutes the third part, and the time at which the Messiah was perceived to have come in the presence of the bread. In other words the whole of *On Pascha* is intended to commemorate and to make present the work of God, the whole is a commemoration, and as such its intent was sacramental. The *aphikoman* could be received in the presence of the risen Jesus, as the voice of the risen Jesus could be heard speaking through Melito as he declaimed: "I am the passover of your salvation." And so the risen Jesus could be known in the sharing of the broken bread.

After this a third cup is permissible, and if the early Christians were anything like the Jews, and anything like modern Christians, it is far from impossible that a further cup (or two!) might be added, and that the celebration might continue until the dawn of the following day.

In conclusion we may understand the outline of *On Pascha* as follows:

Propositio: The scripture has been read, and in the paschal celebration we can come to realize how it is fulfilled.

Narratio: The firstborn of the Egyptians died horribly whilst Israel was liberated. The liberation of Israel is the experience of the Christian through the commemoration of the death of Christ.

Probatio: The whole was the result of Adam's disgrace, as we remember the history of humankind in need of salvation.

Peroratio: Yet the messiah came, and comes to us. In the murder of Christ by Israel, repeating their slaughter of the

[handwritten annotations: "The Last Supper was the fulfillment of the Pascha — for Melito — It was the death of the Lord"]

lamb, is the triumph of God, which in its proclamation is a present reality for us as we celebrate.

On Pascha is itself the text of the liturgy, the means by which the Christians of Sardis, gathered with Melito their bishop, might commemorate and know the presence of Jesus in his triumph.

It may however seem puzzling that there is no eucharistic prayer as such, no direct reference to gifts of bread and wine (the references are there, but indirect), no epiclesis (for all that Melito assumes the activity of the Spirit he does not have a pneumatology as such, as we shall see later in this introduction) and certainly none to the Last Supper. But were Melito to point to the Last Supper he would have been stepping out of his Johannine tradition; there were indeed Quartodecimans who saw the Last Supper as the fulfillment of the Pascha[29] but Melito was not among them. For him the death of the Lord at the same time as, and in place of, the death of the Passover lambs was the fulfillment of the Pascha. There are a number of early prayers for the eucharist or for related table rites which take no account of the last Supper, and Melito's work can stand among them. Certainly it is also (in part at least) a prophetic homily, but the words of Enrico Mazza concerning another description of early Christian worship (Acts 20:9-11) may stand here:

> Paul's words were not just what we could call a homily. It was the liturgical celebration itself, including at the same time liturgical text, proclamation, comment, homily, and physical action, all of which, lasting till dawn, had the characteristics of a vigil.[30]

29 See the citation from Hippolytus, taken from the *Chronicon Paschale*, at pp. 82-83 below.
30 Enrico Mazza, *The Origins of the Eucharistic Prayer* (Collegeville: Liturgical, 1995), 105.

In time this proclamation of God's mighty acts as a means of making them present entered into the eucharistic tradition and is still to be found in liturgies both eastern and western, in the declaration of God's deeds to be found at the beginning of every eucharistic prayer.

The Quartodeciman Pascha and the Jewish Pesah [31]

The reconstruction attempted here depends in part on the assumption that the liturgy of the Quartodecimans followed the broad outlines of the Jewish rite. The basic document for constructing the liturgy of the Jewish Passover at the time of Melito, or more accurately for the period before that of Melito since his liturgy would be formed as much by Christian tradition as by direct Jewish influence, is the Tractate of the Mishnah known as *Pesahim*. Although this is from a later period from that of Melito it does bear traces of more ancient tradition, and there is no doubt that there was a domestic Passover rite of some description before the parting of the Jewish and Christian ways: the *Mishnah* reports the transformation of a rite already in existence rather than creating an entirely new one, a rite which had to undergo some transformation as a result of the destruction of the Temple, but which at the same time required some conformity with the prior ritual.

In broad outline we may suggest that the Jewish ritual which entered the Christian tradition had a setting within a meal, in which context a question is raised from within the group as to the meaning of the actions of which the seder consists. This is answered with reference to Scripture, a retelling of the story of liberation from Egypt. In particular the answer

31 For full details and bibliography on this section see *The Lamb's High Feast,* 31-54, 60-66.

should deal with the lamb, the deliverance from Egypt, the bitter herbs and the unleavened bread. This scriptural retelling is the center of the rite, and is known as the paschal haggadah. The conclusion of the festivity came in the singing of hymns, and perhaps psalms.

We may observe that the second part of *On Pascha* accords with this outline, in that it expounds on liberation from the bondage of sin in answer to a question, whilst dealing with all the set themes, and coming to a hymnic conclusion. The probable point at which this takes place is at the mixing of the second cup of wine and at the time bread is served. Thus we may see the haggadah of the Passover in its context as a repetition of the acts of God in the exodus, taking place over the festal meal. There is no reason to believe that this would be any different for Melito than for his Jewish predecessors, and we must see therefore that *On Pascha* presupposes a table rite.

The haggadah was recited in obedience to the biblical precept to tell of the acts of God in the Passover. It tells of the event which is being celebrated. Likewise the entire festival was celebrated in obedience to biblical command, that the festival was to be a memorial to Israel for ever of the Passover of Egypt. Thus as the function of the haggadah, to tell of the deeds of God, is subsumed into the context of the festival, its function becomes identical with that of the festival, to remember. As remembering is the function of the seder, so the haggadah focuses the act of remembrance. We may suggest that, since the Quartodeciman Passover derives directly from the Jewish celebration, the same motivating factor of remembrance would in some way be transmitted to Christianity. It is on these grounds that the reconstruction of the Quartodeciman liturgy takes the same broad shape as that of Judaism and, we may suggest, has the same fundamental purpose, namely the commemoration of the acts of God.

Support for this view may be gained from noting certain other formal and verbal links between *On Pascha* and the haggadah known in Judaism.

There is a close verbal correspondence between Mishnah *Pesahim* 10.5, which appears in the haggadah, and *On Pascha* 68.

There is the use of the term *aphikomenos* of Christ at *On Pascha* 66 and 86. In these places it is used of Christ in respect of his coming to earth to heal the suffering. This is significant because, as suggested above, it reflects the *aphikoman* of the Jewish Passover rite, a rite which was arguably originally messianic in its significance.

The prescribed shape of the haggadah is, according to the Mishnah, that it should "begin with the disgrace and end with the glory."[32] This is the shape of the second part of *On Pascha*, which begins with Adam's fall and ends with Christ's triumph.

It is on these grounds that a place may be accorded to *On Pascha* within the Quartodeciman liturgy as a Christian haggadah, intending to call to the remembrance of the hearers the mighty work of Christ and to make this work present in their experience. This then allows us to fit the work in with information gathered from elsewhere[33] to give us a clear picture of the celebration known to Melito. In particular however it should be noted that the haggadic parallels fall in the second part of the work; the first belongs to the vigil, the second to the celebration proper.

Melito's anti-Judaism [34]

To our ears Melito's attitude to the Jews is horrifying. In hearing

---

32 Mishnah Pesahim, 10.4.
33 Such as the Syrian *Didascalia* and the *Epistula apostolorum*. The sources are all to be found in translation in this book.
34 For more detail on this subject see the works cited in the bibliography.

what he has to say we should recall that Jews probably out-
numbered Christians in Sardis, and that Melito himself was of
Jewish stock.

A number of factors come into play when Melito deals with
Judaism. Two factors in particular however are predominant.
Firstly we should note that Melito is a Christian standing in the
Johannine tradition. We may note here the consistent
anti-Judaism of John, a Gospel which is also firmly engaged
with Jewish practice: "John is both Jewish and anti-Jewish."[35]
The points made by John are substantially those of Melito; for
Melito, as for John, Christ has superseded the law (John 10:34,
15:25 cf. *On Pascha,* 7, 40-43). The Jews do not listen to Jesus,
nor do they see God in him, whereas the Johannine community
does (so John 1:10-12; 1 John 1:1; John 9 35-41, and perhaps
John 1:45-51; cf. *On Pascha,* 82). The Jews persecute Jesus and
at the last they execute him (John 5:16, 7:1, 8:59 cf. *On Pascha,*
92-93, 96). Both moreover are critical of the Temple, another
point at which there is distance between Johannine Christianity and Judaism (John 2:19-20, 4:21-23 cf. *On Pascha,* 45).
John's attempt to shift the blame for the crucifixion away from
the Romans is brought to an apogee in Melito where they do
not appear at all. It is not Melito but John who is the first to
make the charge of deicide against the Jewish people.[36] The
most recent treatment of this issue concludes that the attitude
of the Johannine Jews towards Jesus is transparent of the attitude felt by John.[37] Essentially it reflects an argument between
a heterodox form of Judaism (Johannine Christianity) and

35 C.K. Barrett, *The Gospel of John and Judaism* (London: SPCK, 1975),
   71. John's anti-Judaism has not gone unnoticed before or since.
36 The phrase of E. Werner "Melito of Sardes, First Poet of Deicide,"
   HUCA 37 (1966), 191-210.
37 John Ashton, *Understanding the Fourth Gospel* (Oxford: Clarendon,
   1991), 131-159.

representatives of what would become mainstream Judaism. The same remains true of Melito's day and situation.

The problem is made more acute by Melito's Quartodecimanism; just as the Quartodecimans at the time of Nicaea were known as Judaizers, so there is a need for Melito's congregation to distinguish itself from the Jews, practicing a similar rite on the same day, albeit apparently at a different time. Just as the Jews were no longer a people, so their Passover was vacuous of meaning now that the true lamb had been slain. John and Melito must distance themselves from the Jewish community precisely because of the proximity of their religious practice. Like Melito, John has a paschal practice close to that of the Jews, and so at 2:13 and 6:4 Pascha is specifically described as being that "of the Jews": that is to say it is distinguished from the Pascha of the Johannine community. The same attitude can be found in the Syrian community producing the *Didascalia,* who are so concerned that their Pascha might be identified with that of the Jews that they actually pray for the annihilation of the Jewish people! On the Jewish side moreover there appears to have been some attempt to put a distance between themselves and Quartodeciman Christians. In particular Nodet and Taylor point to the discussion at *Mishnah Pesahim* 7.1-2 as indicating an attempt to avoid the paschal lamb being roasted in the shape of a cross, and suggest moreover that the prohibition on going on to other parties after midnight in *Mishnah Pesahim* is intended to prevent Jews going on to Christian celebrations[38] (though it is equally likely that in the earliest time the Christians kept Pascha at the same time as the Jewish Pesah, and only later transferred the time of the celebration until after midnight to avoid celebrating at the same time as the Jews.)

38 Étienne Nodet and Justin Taylor, *The Origins of Christianity: An Exploration* (Collegeville: Liturgical, 1998), 352-53; 358-59.

The Theology of Melito

Because *On Pascha* is a liturgical document its interest is primarily liturgical. However a number of other aspects of Melito's thought have been discussed since the discovery of this document.

a) *Melito's doctrine of God in Christ*

Although Origen tells us that Melito thought that God was corporeal, which may be an indication that, like Tertullian, Melito was a stoic,[39] a liturgical and commemorative work like *On Pascha* does not present us with a doctrine of God as such, but rather God is described through his mighty acts of creation and salvation. For Melito, these acts are expressed through Christ made flesh, and Melito's doctrine of Christ as God embodied may be the basis for Origen's claim. We cannot separate Melito's idea of God from his christology which, as an anonymous third century writer has it, proclaims Christ as both God and man.[40]

Bonner, the first editor of *On Pascha*, characterized Melito's christology as essentially a pneumatic christology, and more precisely as a "naive modalism."[41] In other words Bonner felt that Melito did not make a clear distinction between the persons of the Trinity, and thought that Melito believed that Christ was empowered by the Holy Spirit. This was a common idea in the second century, but it is not that of Melito. Melito sees Christ as the creator clothed in flesh. So at *On Pascha*, 66, 86 it is the creator who comes down from

39 This would not be impossible; Melito's treatment of Scripture is reminiscent of the manner in which the stoics discussed ancient literary material. See *The Lamb's High Feast*, 84-92.

40 See Hall, *Melito of Sardis*, xii with reference to Eusebius, *Ecclesiastical History*, 5.28.

41 Bonner, *Homily*, 28.

heaven, and at *On Pascha,* 70 he is enfleshed. *On Pascha,* 47, 66 state that the Lord put on humanity as a garment. Although this is clearly defective by the standards of later centuries, it is orthodox within the context of the second century in that Melito is maintaining the fundamental truths that Jesus Christ was God and that he was flesh. So although Melito's christology may thus conceivably be described as modalist this is not a very helpful definition. His trinitarian theology concentrates on the relationship between the Father and the Son. This is characterized by Hall as "christocentric monotheism"; by this Hall means that for Melito, Christ is God and God is Christ.[42] There is no real distinction between the Father and the Son, indeed at one point we read that Christ is "Insofar as he begets, he is father, insofar as he is begotten, he is Son." Although there has been an attempt to interpret this passage as referring to the sons whom Christ begets in salvation, thinking to rescue Melito from any imputation of heresy, elsewhere we hear that "he bears the father and is borne by him." However strange this may seem to our ears, in the context of the second century this is not heretical. By contrast the Spirit has a limited role to play in *On Pascha.* The Spirit is mentioned four times, at sections 16, 32, 44, 66; these references are to the immortality of the Spirit, which thus protects the Israelite firstborn as a type in the blood, and as the means by which Christ is able to conquer death. We must remember that Melito bears witness to the truth as it was understood in his day and that orthodox faith has been gradually revealed to the church. At the center of the Christian faith stands Christ, and Christ is at the center of the faith proclaimed, lived and celebrated by Melito.

---

42 Hall, "The Christology of Melito: A Misrepresentation Exposed," *Studia Patristica,* 13 (Berlin: Akademie, 1975), 154-168.

b) Eschatology

Eschatology for Melito as we may understand him through
On Pascha is bound up to the liturgical commemoration of the
acts of God, through which God in Christ becomes present in
mind, in prophetic speech, and through the sacramental
agency of the *aphikoman.* The Quartodeciman paschal fast has
an eschatological element, but not simply a future element, but
as related to the meeting of the risen Lord in the assembly.
Other Quartodeciman documents such as *Epistula
Apostolorum*, and indeed the letter of Polycrates, seem to have
a much more futuristic eschatology, and for this reason either
Melito or the other Quartodeciman documents have been
deemed not Quartodeciman. But the difference is more perceived than real for although there are differences of emphasis,
both point to a lively belief in the revelation of the Messiah in
the paschal context. Asia, through its reading of the Apocalypse alongside the fourth Gospel, was an effective incubator
for an eschatological hope, but it is not impossible that Asian
Christianity sustained a lively futuristic eschatological hope
whilst recognizing that the signs of the parousia of Christ were
already present. This tension is present in the fourth Gospel
and is manifest in the statement that "the hour is coming, and
now is, when true worshipers shall worship the father in spirit
and in truth."[43] The realized eschatology which is most prominent in *On Pascha* reflects its liturgical origin, but this is not to
say that Melito would not have been conscious of a futuristic
element also.

A sidelong glance at Quartodeciman eschatology may be
provided in Polycrates' statement that Melito is lying at Sardis
and awaiting the visitation (*episkopê*) from the heavens. When

43 John 4:23.

Polemo, the famous sophist, was dying, and knew moreover that he was dying, he directed that he should be interred alive, so that he should not be found silent. As he was walled up his voice cried out that he should declaim again if he were only to be given a body.[44] Declamation for Polemo was more than a livelihood, it was a life, and the point of life was to declaim. It is in this light that we should understand Polycrates' statement about Melito, who in the resurrection will find fulfillment of his own *episkopê*, rather than the empty hope of Polemo to have a body in order to declaim once again.

c) *Typology*

In *On Pascha* Melito presents us with an exegetical method which may be termed "historical typology": the events of the Old Testament are seen to be typified in the New Testament, and there is a correlation seen between the Old Testament events of liberation and the New Testament events of salvation. The events of *Exodus* are described as types (*tupoi*), a word which is also employed by Justin and Barnabas, although there are certainly differences between Melito's use of the term and that of his contemporaries. The word appears in the Pauline correspondence, but the theory itself as presented by Melito has more in common with John than with Paul. Melito has a theory of typology according to which the type, say the first Passover, precedes the reality, the salvation worked by Jesus, which fulfils it. A very similar typological scheme may be seen at work in the fourth Gospel; for instance the descent of the manna given to the Israelites in the wilderness is a type of Christ's descent as a gift of salvation. In John the law had grace in itself; the grace brought by Christ may be such as to outweigh it, and in outweighing to invalidate it, but this does not mean that it had no

44 Philostratus, *Lives of the Sophists*, 1.544.

validity on its own. In this context we may note the intrusion of
"true" (*alêthinos*) in John 6:32; this is reflected by the word
which Melito employs to describe the reality as opposed to the
type, *alêtheia.* Whereas the law was given by Moses, grace and
truth came through Jesus Christ. Both the thought and the language here are as much Melito's as they are John's.[45] According to Melito's theory the types are temporary in effect. Thus the
blood of the paschal lamb is a type, or prefiguration, of the
blood of Christ, as is the law of the Gospel. The sufferings of the
just, like Abel and Joseph, are types of the sufferings of
Christ.[46] Melito compares these types to sculptors' working
models, and to metaphors: they are of use only until the finished
work has been made. The people of Israel are as the artist's
model, a preliminary sketch for the Church. The Law is the metaphor by which the Gospel is elucidated.[47]

But apart from its Johannine roots, Melito's theory of
typology may also owe something to a common fund of philosophical wisdom. The process by which events in history occur beforehand as types which are ultimately fulfilled, so making it possible for the event to be interpreted in the light of the
prefiguration, leads Melito to state that there are specific and
proper times for each stage of this process. The extended image of the preliminary sketch is taken from sculpture, but this
may be a pedagogic explanation of an interpretative theory
which has already come to him in a developed form. This view
is not, however, explicit in Melito. Melito's philosophical
knowledge is that of the stoic interpreter of Homer. In the time
of Melito the subject of allegorization both of ancient religious
myth and of poetry was a live one. May we not see Melito's

45 So compare *On Pascha,* 7 with John 1:17
46 *On Pascha,* 59.
47 *On Pascha,* 40.

typological system in this context, as a response to the debate about the value and function of allegorical interpretation in the rhetorical schools? Not, of course, that his theory is identical to any of those produced by the pagan thinkers, but that he sees himself in a similar context, both in interpreting an authoritative text and in interpreting its religious content. It is highly unlikely that Melito in Sardis could have been unaware of the debate. He would naturally read the scripture in the way in which Cornutus, the stoic interpreter of Homeric myth, read the poets, as a riddle which hides a wisdom. The wisdom, for Melito, would be the eternal wisdom of God. The typological method would be the means by which the riddle is understood. Apart, however, from the Melito's use of the image of the sculptors' working models,[48] there is a significant difference between Melito and his pagan contemporaries in their attitudes to history. Whereas the pagans differed in the extent to which they would consider the events described to be historical, this consideration was not of central relevance to their treatments of the texts. On the whole the literal meaning is to be altogether rejected. This is certainly true of Heraclitus, to an extent of Plutarch, and apparently the meaning of Cornutus and of Maximus of Tyre (although this is not explicitly stated).[49] Whereas for Melito the significance of the events he describes inheres in their historical character. Had they not taken place then his theory of typology would not be possible. The literal meaning is no longer significant, but it is not simply a construction to hide a greater intended significance. The metaphor is understood in the light of the gospel which is the reality to

---

48 Quintilian frequently employs the image of the sculptor and the statue for the construction of a speech by an orator, but does not make use of the idea of working models.
49 See the discussion at *The Lamb's High Feast*, 84-92.

which the metaphor points, but the metaphor must retain its own literal and historical significance in order to be an effective metaphor pointing to a greater reality. This is in line with the argument of Quintilian that historical narratives are to be preferred to those which are fictitious or merely realistic, since the force of such a narrative is in proportion to its truth.[50] Melito is thus a clear example of a practitioner of a typology in which the place of history is significant, and in this lies a significant difference between Melito's treatment of his authoritative text and that of his pagan contemporaries. In essence however he is doing much the same as his contemporaries whilst at the same time differentiating himself from them, in much the same way that he is liturgically acting in a way much like that of the Jews whilst putting distance between himself and them.

Conclusion: Melito's liturgical theology

Although Melito himself would not think in the categories in which we think, we can justly understand him from within the framework of liturgical theology. *On Pascha* is a liturgical document, and in the light of the Jewish understanding of remembrance as a means of making the past a present reality, and bringing to bear the blessings of the past in the hope of the future, as in the light of Hellenistic theories about the way in which rhetoric might bring to life in the minds and ears of the audience a reality not present, we may understand that for Melito and for his hearers the liturgy was the point at which the glory of God in Jesus Christ, the resurrection triumph and the pains of the passion, the mysteries proclaimed by the Scriptures and the experience of salvation now and in the future

50 Quintilian, *Institutio Oratoria*, 2.4.2.

came to life and reality. In proclamation both of scriptural past and prophetic present, in the presence of Christ in the sacramentally transformed rite of *aphikoman* and in his prophetic voice, in the experience of rejoicing after vigil and fasting, in the light suffusing the paschal night from full moon and kindled lamps, Melito and his congregation met their Lord and were enabled to proclaim his eternal triumph in an eternal commemoration.

Melito of Sardis
ON PASCHA

1) The Scripture of the exodus of the Hebrews has been read,
and the words of the mystery have been declared;[1]
how the sheep was sacrificed,
and how the people was saved,
and how Pharaoh was flogged by the mystery.

2) Therefore, well-beloved, understand,
how the mystery of the Pascha
is both new and old,
eternal and provisional,
perishable and imperishable,
mortal and immortal.

3) It is old with respect to the law,
new with respect to the word.
Provisional with respect to the type,[2]

---

1 The meaning of this opening phrase has been much debated. In particular
two assertions have been made which affect its interpretation:
   a) That the Scripture was read in Hebrew and
   b) That the second line refers to another process intervening between
the reading and the delivery of *On Pascha*, for instance a translation of
the Hebrew text (on the assumption that the text was read in Hebrew) or
else a preliminary treatment (something like the *enarratio*, which was a
standard practice of the schools after a reading).
   The translation here reflects the belief that neither assertion is true.
The Scripture was not read in Hebrew (the exodus is that "of the Hebrews" and not "in Hebrew") and the second line is a couplet lending so-
lemnity to the description of the proceedings. *On Pascha*, or at least part
of *On Pascha*, is the *enarratio*, as Melito himself makes clear. For details
of the discussion and bibliography see Alistair Stewart-Sykes, *The
Lamb's High Feast*, 96-9, 172-76.
2 The word here rendered "type" is intended by Melito to indicate that the

yet everlasting through grace.
It is perishable because of the slaughter of the sheep,
imperishable because of the life of the Lord.
It is mortal because of the burial in the ground,
immortal because of the resurrection from the dead.

4) For the law is old,
but the word is new.
The type is provisional,
but grace is everlasting.
The sheep is perishable,
but the Lord,
not broken as a lamb but raised up as God,
is imperishable.
For though led to the slaughter like a sheep,
he was no sheep.
Though speechless as a lamb,
neither yet was he a lamb.
For there was once a type, but now the reality has appeared.

5) For instead of the lamb there was a son,
and instead of the sheep a man;
in the man was Christ encompassing all things.

6) So the slaughter of the sheep,
and the sacrificial procession of the blood,
and the writing of the law encompass Christ,
on whose account everything in the previous law took place,
though better in the new dispensation.

7) For the law was a word,
and the old was new,

events of the old covenant are models of what would occur under the new
covenant. He explains his theory of typology below at sections 34-45.
The word is used by many patristic writers, but precise understandings
of the relationship between the type and the reality, or fulfillment, vary.
In essence the idea of typology is that the events of the old covenant
were intended to lead to the greater perfection of the new covenant. See
above, pp. 31-4.

going out from Sion and Jerusalem,
and the commandment was grace,
and the type was a reality,
and the lamb was a son,
and the sheep was a man,
and the man was God.

8) For he was born a son,
and led as a lamb,
and slaughtered as a sheep,
and buried as a man,
and rose from the dead as God,
being God by his nature and a man.

9) He is all things.
He is law, in that he judges.
He is word, in that he teaches.
He is grace, in that he saves.
He is father, in that he begets.[3]

He is son, in that he is begotten.
He is sheep, in that he suffers.
He is human, in that he is buried.
He is God, in that he is raised up.

10) This is Jesus the Christ,
to whom be the glory for ever and ever. Amen.[4]

3 Note that Christ himself is described here as father! This is an example of
the naive modalism, or better christocentric monotheism, espoused by
Melito. In time modalism became recognized as heretical because of its
inadequacies, but it would be unreasonable to apply such a title to Melito,
in whose period the complexities of Trinitarian relationships had not
been discussed. For further discussion of Melito's christology see the introduction above, pp. 28-9.

4 This doxology divides off the first portion of the work. As was observed
in the introduction, in Graeco-Roman rhetoric it was usual to start by setting out what the speech would achieve in a section known as the *thesis* or
propositio. In this opening Melito sets out the fundamental theme of *On
Pascha*, namely the substitution of the Christian Pascha for the Jewish
Pesah through the resurrection triumph of Jesus.

II. Narratio

11) This is the mystery of the Pascha,
just as it is written in the law, which was read a little
while ago.
I shall narrate the scriptural story,[5]
how he gave command to Moses in Egypt,
when wanting to flog Pharaoh
and to free Israel from flogging
through the hand of Moses.

12) "Look," he says, "you shall take a lamb, without spot
or blemish,
and, toward the evening, slaughter it with the sons of Israel.
And eat it at night with haste.
And not a bone of it shall you break."

13) "This is what you shall do," he says:
"You shall eat it in one night by families and tribes,
with your loins girded up
and with staves in your hands.
This is the Passover of the Lord,
a commemoration to the sons of Israel for ever."

14) "Taking the blood of the sheep
you shall anoint the front doors of your houses
putting blood on the doorposts of the entrances;
the sign of the blood to avert the angel.
For behold, I shall strike Egypt
and in one night shall both beast and man be made childless."

15) Then Moses, having slaughtered the sheep
and performed the mystery at night with the sons of Israel,[6]

5 By stating that he will tell the story from Scripture, Melito is informing his
   audience that the part of his speech which is now beginning is the *diêgêma*,
   or *narratio*, the narrative which lays down the basis for the remainder of
   the speech (the confirmation or denial). Beyond this however we must note
   that in Scripture the telling of the works of God is a significant part of
   praise. Melito unites the scriptural tradition with that of classical rhetoric
   by giving praise whilst laying down the *narratio* of his declamation.
6 Although this language is obviously redolent of the mystery religions,
   more influential is Melito's own experience of a nocturnal commemoration.

sealed the doors of the houses to protect the people
and to avert the angel.[7]

16) But while the sheep is being slaughtered,
and the Pascha is being eaten,
and the mystery is completed,
and the people is rejoicing,
and Israel is being sealed:
then came the angel to strike Egypt,
those uninitiated in the mystery,
those with no part in the Pascha,
those not sealed by the blood,
those not guarded by the spirit,
the hostile,
the faithless;
in one night he struck them and made them childless.

17) For the angel had passed by Israel,
and seen him sealed with the blood of the sheep,
he fell upon Egypt,
he tamed stiff-necked Pharaoh with grief,
clothing him not with a garment of gray,
nor with a tunic all torn,
but with all Egypt torn and grieving for her first-born.

---

7 This passage is full of allusions to Exodus 12 but is very much a free retelling, far freer than the targums, or Jewish translations of the Scriptures, which were in contemporary use. The instruction not to break a
bone of the animal was clearly significant in the light of the Johannine association of Jesus and the Passover lamb, since John quotes the same text
in referring to the death of Jesus at the time the lambs were being slaughtered in the Temple (John 19:36). Although Melito renders Exodus very
freely here, this instruction is found in the Septuagint in a very different
place from that of the Hebrew text. Therefore Melito here would seem
either to be using a Hebrew text or another Greek translation, but not the
Septuagint. In describing the Pascha as an apotropaic rite, Melito insinu-
ates much language relating to Christian initiation. One should not however conclude from this language that initiation was necessarily practiced at Pascha in Melito's time.

18) For all Egypt was pained and grieving,
in tears and mourning,
and came to Pharaoh stricken with woe,
not outwardly only but inwardly.
Not only were her garments torn,
but also her delicate breasts.

19) It was indeed a strange spectacle,
here people beating their breasts, there people wailing,
and grief-stricken Pharaoh in the middle,
seated on sackcloth and ashes,
palpable darkness thrown around him as a mourning cloak,
clad in all Egypt like a tunic of grief.[8]

20) For Egypt was surrounding Pharaoh
like a robe of wailing.
Such a tunic was woven for the tyrannical body,
With such a garment did the angel of justice
clothe unyielding Pharaoh:
bitter grief and palpable darkness
and a strange childlessness, the loss of her first-born.

21) The death of the first-born was swift and greedy,
it was a strange trophy on which to gaze,
upon those falling dead in one moment.
And the food of death was the defeat of the prostrate.

22) Listen and wonder at a new disaster,
for these things enclosed the Egyptians:
long night,
palpable darkness,
death grasping,
the angel squeezing out the life,
and Hades gulping down the first-born.[9]

8   The theatrical imagery employed here is common in the rhetoric of the
    second century. Pharaoh is depicted as a tragic figure, surrounded by the
    chorus, the people of Egypt.
9   The description of death grasping the firstborn is, according to Thomas

23) But the strangest and most terrifying thing you are yet
to hear:
In the palpable darkness hid untouchable death,
and the wretched Egyptians were grasping the darkness,
while death sought out and grasped the Egyptian first-born
at the angel's command.[10]

24) If anyone grasped the darkness
he was pulled away by death.
And one of the first-born,
grasping the material darkness in his hand,
as his life was stripped away,
cried out in distress and terror:
"Whom does my hand hold?
Whom does my soul dread?
Who is the dark one enfolding my whole body?
If it is a father, help me.
If it is a mother, comfort me.
If it is a brother, speak to me.
If it is a friend, support me.
If it is an enemy, depart from me, for I am a first-born."

25) Before the first-born fell silent, the long silence held
him and spoke to him:
"You are my first-born,

Halton, "Stylistic Device in Melito *Peri Pascha*," in *Kyriakon: Festschrift
Johannes Quasten,* ed. Patrick Granfield and Josef A. Jungmann (Münster:
Aschendorff, 1970), 249-255, reminiscent of Homer's description of
blinded cyclops grasping for his victims. In Melito's use of the word
katapinô to describe the manner in which Hades swallows the first-born
we may perhaps also discern echoes of Hesiod's description of Kronos
swallowing his offspring.

10 On this passage Karl Gerlach, *The Ante-Nicene Pascha: A Rhetorical
History* (Leuven: Peeters, 1998), 64-5 comments: "The 'grasping darkness' is not just melodrama, but embraces the delivery of the homily in a
dark place where Christians have gathered on the paschal night with only
a few candles or torches for light. Rhetorically, Melito's hearers are being killed off one by one, except for the sign of blood."

I am your destiny, the silence of death."[11]

26) Another first-born, perceiving the seizure of the
first-born,
denied himself, so not bitterly to die:
"I am not a first-born,
I was begotten third."
But the one who could not be deceived fastened on the
first-born
who fell silently down.
At one moment the first-born fruit of the Egyptians was
destroyed,
the first-begotten, the first-born,
not human only but of dumb beasts,
the desired,
the fondled one, was dashed downward.

27) A lowing was heard in the plains of the land,
the moaning of beasts over their sucklings,
the cow with sucking calf and the horse with foal,
and the rest of the beasts bearing young and carrying milk,
and their moaning over their first-born
was bitter and piteous.

28) At the human loss there was howling and grief
over the dead first-born,
and all Egypt was stinking with unburied bodies.

29) It was a terrible spectacle to watch,
the mothers of the Egyptians with hair undone,
the fathers with minds undone,
wailing terribly in the Egyptian tongue:
"By evil chance we are bereaved in a moment of our
first-born issue."

11 Here is another classical reference, this time to Aeschylus, *Eumenides*,
935; it is not coincidental that the allusion is from a theatrical piece, since
the manner in which Melito self-consciously stands as reporter is rather
like that of a messenger-speech in Greek tragedy.

They were beating their breasts,
they were tapping time with their hands for the dance of
the dead.

30) Such was the calamity which surrounded Egypt,
and made her suddenly childless.
Israel was guarded by the slaughter of the sheep,
and was illuminated by the shedding of blood,
and the death of the sheep was a wall for the people.

31) O strange and ineffable mystery!
The slaughter of the sheep was Israel's salvation,
and the death of the sheep was life for the people,
and the blood averted the angel.

32) Tell me angel, what turned you away?[12]
The slaughter of the sheep or the life of the Lord?
The death of the sheep or the type of the Lord?
The blood of the sheep or the spirit of the Lord?

33) It is clear that you turned away
seeing the mystery of the Lord in the sheep
and the life of the Lord in the slaughter of the sheep
and the type of the Lord in the death of the sheep.
Therefore you struck not Israel down,
but made Egypt alone childless.

34) What is this strange mystery,
that Egypt is struck down for destruction
and Israel is guarded for salvation?
Listen to the meaning of the mystery.[13]

---

12 The sudden address to the angel is again typical of rhetorical practice at
the time of Melito.

13 The word translated here as "meaning," *dunamis*, is employed by rhetorical
writers to mean the persuasive effect of oratory, (Lucian, *How to write History*, 34) or of individual units of a speech such as the choice of sounds (so
Quintilian, *Instituto Oratoria*, II.15.3-4, with reference to ps-Isocrates;
Dionysius of Halicarnassus, *On Composition*, 12). The source of this usage is probably Plato, who discusses the *dunamis* of words with reference
to their construction (*Cratylus*, 394B). What follows does not fit into the

35) Nothing, beloved, is spoken or made without an
analogy and a sketch;
for everything which is made and spoken has its analogy,
what is spoken an analogy, what is made a prototype,
so that whatever is made may be perceived through the
prototype
and whatever is spoken clarified by the illustration.

36) This is what occurs in the case of a first draft;
it is not a finished work but exists so that, through the
model,
that which is to be can be seen.
Therefore a preliminary sketch is made of what is to be,
from wax or from clay or from wood,
so that what will come about,
taller in height,
and greater in strength,
and more attractive in shape,
and wealthier in workmanship,
can be seen through the small and provisional sketch.

37) When the thing comes about of which the sketch was
a type,
that which was to be, of which the type bore the likeness,
then the type is destroyed, it has become useless,
it yields up the image to what is truly real.
What was once valuable becomes worthless,
when what is of true value appears.

38) To each then is its own time:
the type has its own time,
the material has its own time,
the reality has its own time.

rhetorical plan of *On Pascha* but casts light nonetheless on what has pre-
ceded and what follows. Such a digression was common in the rhetoric of
Melito's period; it was meant to sustain the interest of the audience and,
whilst being a digression, nonetheless to relate to the main content of the
speech. This is true of Melito's digression here.

When you construct the model you require it,
because in it you can see the image of what is to be.
You prepare the material before the model,
you require it because of what will come about from it.
You complete the work, and that alone you require,
that alone you desire,
because only there can you see the type, and the material,
and the reality.

39) So then, just as with the provisional examples,
so it is with eternal things;
as it is with things on earth,
so it is with the things in heaven.
For indeed the Lord's salvation and his truth were
prefigured in the people,
and the decrees of the Gospel were proclaimed in advance
by the law.

40) Thus the people was a type, like a preliminary sketch,
and the law was the writing of an analogy.
The Gospel is the narrative and fulfillment of the law,
and the church is the repository of reality.

41) So the type was valuable in advance of the reality,
and the illustration was wonderful before its elucidation.
So the people were valuable before the church arose,
and the law was wonderful before the illumination of the
Gospel.

42) But when the church arose and the Gospel came to be,
the type, depleted, gave up meaning to the truth:
and the law, fulfilled, gave up meaning to the Gospel.

43) In the same way that the type is depleted,
conceding the image to what is intrinsically real,
and the analogy is brought to completion through the
elucidation of interpretation,
so the law is fulfilled by the elucidation of the Gospel,

and the people is depleted by the arising of the church,
and the model is dissolved by the appearance of the Lord.
And today those things of value are worthless,
since the things of true worth have been revealed.

44) For then the slaughter of the sheep was of value,
now it is worthless because of the Lord's life.
The death of the sheep was of value,
now it is worthless because of the Lord's salvation.
The blood of the sheep was of value,
now it is worthless because of the Lord's spirit.
The dumb lamb was of value,
now it is worthless because of the son without spot.
The temple below was of value,
now it is worthless because of the heavenly Christ.

45) The Jerusalem below was of value,
now it is worthless because of the heavenly Jerusalem.
Once the narrow inheritance was of value,
now it is worthless because of the breadth of grace.
For it is not on one place, nor in a narrow plot, that the
glory of God is established,
but on all the ends of the earth.[14]
For his grace has been poured out
and the almighty God has made his dwelling there.
Through Christ Our Lord,
to whom be the glory for ever and ever. Amen

46) You have heard the narrative of the type and its
correspondence:
hear now the confirmation of the mystery.[15]

14 The polemic against the Temple, whilst derived from Johannine tradition
(note in particular John 2:19-21, which associates the true Temple with
the body of Christ), is particularly pointed here because the slaughter of
the paschal lambs was restricted to the Temple, whereas Melito is suggesting that the death of Christ has significance throughout the world.
15 Narrative (*diêgêma*) and confirmation (*kataskeuê*) are two parts of a normal speech in the Greek world. Melito alerted us earlier to the narratio,

Confirmation

What is the Pascha?[16]
It is called by its name because of what constitutes it:
from "suffer" comes "suffering."[17]
Therefore learn who is the suffering one, and who shares
in the suffering one's suffering,
and why the Lord is present on the earth to surround
himself with the suffering one,
and take him to the heights of the heavens.

47) God, in the beginning,
having made the heaven and the earth and all in them
through the Word,
formed humanity from the earth and shared his own breath.
He set him in the garden in the east, in Eden,
there to rejoice.
There he laid down for him the law, through his
commandment:
"Eat food from all the trees in the garden
yet eat not from the tree of the knowledge of good and evil;
on the day that you eat you shall die."

and now informs us that its confirmation will follow. The confirmation
was intended to show the true meaning, and veracity, of the preceding narrative. Melito follows the pattern of *diêgêma-kataskeuê*, but does not simply follow it woodenly. Note that the narrative is of the type, whereas the
demonstration is of the reality which the type represented, that is to say the
true foundation of the mystery is the salvation wrought in Christ. This may
accord to the pattern of the paschal vigil of the Quartodecimans, with the
fasting gathering in darkness concentrating on the old model of the Pascha
(at the time at which the Jews are keeping festival) and the following festivity, probably at midnight, centring on the fulfillment wrought in Christ.

16 Rhetorical questions were common enough in Asian Greek rhetoric; this
question however at this point has a particular significance since it corre-
sponds in the liturgical action to the point at which the questions are asked
in the Jewish Passover, in keeping with the direction at Exodus 12:26.

17 This line is untranslatable; the rendition here is that of Hall, *Melito of
Sardis on Pascha* 23. The line cannot be rendered into English because it
depends on the similarity of the two, unrelated, words *Pascha* and
paschein, the latter of which means "to suffer."

48) The man was susceptible by nature of good and evil,
as a clod of earth may receive seed of either kind,
and he consented to the wicked and seductive counselor,
and stretched out for the tree and broke the commandment
and disobeyed God.
For this was he thrown out into this world, condemned as
though to prison.

49) This man became fecund and long-lived,
yet through tasting of the tree he was destroyed,
and was dissolved into the earth.
He left an inheritance to his children,
and as an inheritance he left his children:
not purity but lust,
not incorruption but decay,
not honor but dishonor,
not freedom but bondage,
not sovereignty but tyranny,
not life but death,
not salvation but destruction.

50) Strange and terrible was the destruction of people on earth,
for these things attended them:
they were grasped by tyrannical sin
and they were led to the land of sensuality,
where they were swamped in unsatisfying pleasures:
by adultery,
by lust,
by license,
by love of money,
by murder,
by the shedding of blood,
by the tyranny of evil,
by the tyranny of lawlessness.

51) The father took up sword against his son,
and the son laid hands upon his father

and impiously struck the breasts which fed him.
And brother killed brother,
and host harmed guest,
and friend murdered friend,
and man struck down man with a tyrannical right hand.
Everyone became murderers,
parricides,
infanticides,
fratricides, everyone on earth. [18]

52) The strangest and most terrible thing happened on the earth:
a mother touched the flesh which she had borne,
and fastened onto those she had fed at the breast;
and the fruit of her loins she received in her loins,
becoming a terrible tomb, the wretched mother
gobbling up, not gabbling to, what she had borne.

53) Many other bizarre and most terrible and dissolute things took place among people:
a father went to bed with his child,
a son with his mother,
and a brother with his sister and a male with a male,
and each was braying for his neighbor's wife.

54) Sin rejoiced in all of this,
working together with death,
making forays into human souls
and preparing the bodies of the dead as his food.
Sin set his sign on every one

18 Both scriptural narratives and Greek mythology provide the basis for this account. As a decline narrative, it is a typical device of rhetoricians and philosophers of the period. We may compare in particular ps-Anarcharsis, *Letter* 9: "Long ago the earth was the common possession of god and of people. In time however they transgressed, dedicating to the Gods as their own territory what was the common possession of all. The gods, in return for this, gave fitting gifts in return: strife, desire for pleasure, meanness of spirit. As these things mixed and separated there grew up all the evils which affect all mortals..."

and those on whom he etched his mark were doomed to death.
55) All flesh fell under sin,
and every body under death,
and every soul was plucked from its dwelling of flesh,
and that which was taken from the dust was reduced to dust,
and the gift of God was locked away in Hades.
What was marvelously knit together was unraveled,
and the beautiful body divided.

56) Humanity was doled out by death,
for a strange disaster and captivity surrounded him;
he was dragged off a captive under the shadow of death,
and the father's image was left desolate.

For this reason in the body of the Lord
is the paschal mystery completed.

57) The Lord made advance preparation for his own suffering,
in the patriarchs and in the prophets and in the whole people;
through the law and the prophets he sealed them.
That which more recently and most excellently came to pass
he arranged from of old.
For when it would come to pass it would find faith,
having been foreseen of old.[19]

58) Thus the mystery of the Lord,
prefigured from of old through the vision of a type,
is today fulfilled and has found faith,
even though people think it something new.
For the mystery of the Lord is both new and old;
old with respect to the law,
but new with respect to grace.
But if you scrutinize the type through its outcome you
will discern him.

59) Thus if you wish to see the mystery of the Lord,
look at Abel who is likewise slain,
at Isaac who is likewise tied up,[20]

19 Cf. Justin, *I Apol* 33.2.
20 There is a tradition in Judaism concerning Isaac's sacrifice as a redemptive

at Joseph who is likewise traded,
at Moses who is likewise exposed,
at David who is likewise hunted down,
at the prophets who likewise suffer for the sake of Christ.

60) And look at the sheep, slaughtered in the land of Egypt, which saved Israel through its blood whilst Egypt was struck down.

61) The Mystery of the Lord is proclaimed through the prophetic voice.
For Moses says to the people:
"And you shall look upon your life hanging before your eyes night and day and you will not have faith in your life."[21]

62) David says:
"Why have the nations been haughty, and the peoples imagined vain things?
The kings of the earth stood by and the rulers gathered themselves together
against the Lord and against his anointed one."[22]

63) Jeremiah says:
"I am like a harmless lamb led to sacrifice;
they planned evil for me saying: come let us put wood on his bread and let us rub him out from the land of the living. And his name shall not be remembered."[23]

64) Isaiah says:
"Like a sheep he was led to slaughter and like a silent lamb before its shearer he does not open his mouth; who shall tell of his generation?"[24]

---

offering; it is possible to perceive an allusion to this here, where Isaac's suffering is seen as a type of that of Christ. See fragments 9-11 below for further discussion and bibliography.

21 Deuteronomy 28:66.
22 Psalm 2:1-2.
23 Jeremiah 11:19.
24 Isaiah 53:7-8. Note that this collection of proof-texts stands at the conclusion

65) Many other things were proclaimed by many prophets
concerning the mystery of the Pascha, who is Christ,
to whom be the glory for ever.
Amen.[25]

III — *Peroratio*

66) This is the one who comes from heaven onto the earth
for the suffering one,
and wraps himself in the suffering one through a virgin
womb,[26]
and comes as a man.
He accepted the suffering of the suffering one,
through suffering in a body which could suffer,
and set free the flesh from suffering.
Through the spirit which cannot die
he slew the manslayer death.

of what is effectively the *probatio* of Melito's declaration and thus con-
tributes to the proof by means of citation; this procedure is typical of the
schools, but is also consonant with the practice of Christian prophecy,
where every prophecy required proof, which might be supplied by show-
ing it to be consonant with the Scriptures. It is possible that these prophetic scriptures had been read at the paschal vigil.

25 With this doxology the *probatio* ends. Melito has shown how good and
right it is that in the mercy of God the Pascha should be kept. He now
turns to his *peroratio*, bringing together all the themes of his discourse,
praising God, and making the salvation worked by God at Pascha a reality for his audience.

26 The word for suffering is here *paschon*. The connection is being made
still between Jesus and the paschal lamb. This is particularly significant
in that the word used for Jesus' coming is *aphikomenos*. This is reminiscent of the word *aphikoman*, a portion of bread broken off from the main
loaf at the Passover seder of Judaism, and hidden. In modern Judaism the
finding of the *aphikoman* is considered a children's game, but according
to Daube the *aphikoman* was originally a messianic symbol, and was intended to indicate the coming of the Messiah. Here the identification of
aphikoman and Jesus as Messiah are tied together; we may suggest moreover that here begins the liturgical climax, and that at this point in the
seder the *aphikoman* is revealed, identified with the Messiah, with Jesus
and through Jesus with the paschal lamb. See in particular on this David
Daube, *He That Cometh* (London: Diocese of London, 1966).

67) He is the one led like a lamb
and slaughtered like a sheep;
he ransomed us from the worship of the world
as from the land of Egypt,
and he set us free from the slavery of the devil
as from the hand of Pharaoh,
and sealed our souls with his own spirit,
and the members of our body with his blood.[27]

68) This is the one who clad death in shame
and, as Moses did to Pharaoh,
made the devil grieve.
This is the one who struck down lawlessness
and made injustice childless,
as Moses did to Egypt.
This is the one who delivered us from slavery to freedom,
from darkness into light,
from death into life,
from tyranny into an eternal Kingdom,[28]
and made us a new priesthood,
and a people everlasting for himself.

27 Note the association of the spirit and the blood of Christ, similar to that made by Apollinarius, Melito's Asian contemporary, who identifies the water and the blood which flowed from the side of Christ with his word and his spirit (see the citation from Apollinarius at p. 81-2 below; note also 1 John 5:6-8). It would be mistaken to see a reference to baptism here, for although there is some baptismal language, such as the references to sealing with the blood of the lamb, the fact that according to Melito the doorposts are "anointed," and the shedding of blood "illuminates" Israel, this is imagery and does not imply that baptism occurred at this liturgical occasion. On the matter of paschal baptism see S.G. Hall "Paschal Baptism," *Studia Evangelica*, 6 (TU 112; Berlin, Akademie, 1973), 239-51.

28 The close similarity between this passage and *Mishnah Pesahim* 10.5, which is part of the paschal haggadah, is particularly significant. This was one of the parallels which first alerted scholars to the possibility that *On Pascha* might be a Christian Paschal haggadah. The passage from *Mishnah Pesahim* runs: He brought us out from bondage to freedom, from sorrow to gladness and from mourning to a festival day, and from darkness to a great light and from tyranny to redemption...

69) This is the Pascha of our salvation:
this is the one who in many people endured many things.
This is the one who was murdered in Abel,
tied up in Isaac,
exiled in Jacob,
sold in Joseph,
exposed in Moses,
slaughtered in the lamb,
hunted down in David,
dishonored in the prophets.

70) This is the one made flesh in a virgin,
who was hanged on a tree,
who was buried in the earth,
who was raised from the dead,
who was exalted to the heights of heaven.[29]

71) This is the lamb slain,
this is the speechless lamb,
this is the one born of Mary the fair ewe,
this is the one taken from the flock,
and led to slaughter.
Who was sacrificed in the evening,
and buried at night;
who was not broken on the tree,
who was not undone in the earth,
who rose from the dead and resurrected humankind from
the grave below.

72) This is the one who has been murdered.
And where murdered?
In the middle of Jerusalem.[30]

---

29 This emphasis on the exalted Christ is again surely reminiscent of the
   Johannine tradition, not simply of the visions in Revelation but of the ex-
   altation tradition underlying John's Gospel, where, throughout the fare-
   well discourses Jesus talks of glorification without mentioning
   resurrection.
30 Although it has been argued (by A.E. Harvey "Melito and Jerusalem"

By whom? By Israel.[31]
Why? Because he healed their lame,
and cleansed their lepers,
and enlightened their blind,
and raised up their dead;
and therefore he died.
Where is it written in the law and the prophets:
"They repaid me bad things for good and childlessness for
my soul.
They planned wickedness for me saying:
'Let us tie up the just man because he is a nuisance to us'"?

73) What strange injustice have you done, O Israel?
You have dishonored the one who honored you,
you have disgraced the one who glorified you,
you have denied the one who owned you,
you have ignored the one who made you known,
you have murdered the one who gave you life.

Journal of Theological Studies, ns 17 [1966], 401-40), that Melito places
the crucifixion in the middle of Jerusalem, rather than outside the walls
as the Gospels state, because the site of the crucifixion (now the Church
of the Holy Sepulchre) was in the middle of Jerusalem after the resiting
of the walls of the city early in the second century, this is more probably a
theological statement resulting from the identification of the death of
Christ with that of the lambs in the Temple. That Mount Moriah, where
Isaac was offered, was subsequently identified in the Jewish tradition
with the Temple mount, would tend to lend support to this interpretation.
31 The manner in which Melito blames Israel entirely for the events of the
passion, without mention of the Romans, is shared with the similarly
Quartodeciman *Gospel of Peter*. Whereas Melito may be concerned not
to alienate the Roman state, it is more probable that the blame of Israel
derives from his Johannine theological tradition, whose social situation
and need to distinguish itself from Judaism closely mirrors that of Melito
himself. Post-holocaust commentators have picked up strongly on
Melito's anti-Judaism here. We should note however that the anti-Judaism
is a counterpoint to the acts of God, and to the salvation of the gentiles.
Melito himself would not have identified it as a theme in his work, however prominent this section is in modern discussion. For further discussion
and bibliography, see the introduction above.

74) O Israel, what have you done?
Is it not written for you: "You shall not spill innocent blood"
so that you might not die the death of the wicked?
"I" said Israel. "I killed the Lord."
Why? "Because he had to die."
You have erred, O Israel, to reason so
about the slaughter of the Lord.

75) He had to suffer, but not through you.
He had to be dishonored, but not by you.
He had to be judged, but not by you.
he had to be hung up, but not by you and by your right hand.

76) This, O Israel, is the cry with which you should have called to God:
"O master, if your son should suffer,
and this is your will,
let him suffer indeed, but not by me.
Let him suffer through foreigners,
let him be judged by the uncircumcised,
let him be nailed in place by a tyrannical right hand,
not mine."

77) With this cry, O Israel, you did not call out to God.
Nor did you devote yourself to the master,
nor did you have regard for his works.

78) You did not have regard for the withered hand restored to its body,
nor the eyes of the maimed opened by a hand,
nor limp bodies made strong through a voice.
Nor did you regard the strangest of signs,
a corpse four days dead called alive from a tomb.[32]

32 Melito's emphasis on the signs of Jesus' activity (*sêmeia*) is again reminiscent of the Johannine tradition.

79) You put these things to one side,
you hurried to the slaughter of the Lord.
You prepared for him sharp nails and false witnesses,
and ropes and whips,
and vinegar and gall,
and a sword and torture as against a murderous thief.
You brought forth a flogging for his body,
and thorns for his head;
and you bound his goodly hands,
which formed you from the earth.
And you fed with gall his goodly mouth which fed you
with life.
And you killed your Lord at the great feast.[33]

80) And while you were rejoicing he was starving.
You were drinking wine and eating bread;
he had vinegar and gall.
Your face was bright whereas his was cast down.
You were triumphant while he was afflicted.
You were making music while he was being judged.
You were proposing toasts;
he was being nailed in place.
You were dancing, he was buried.
You were reclining on a cushioned couch,
he in grave and coffin.[34]

33 Technically this would mean the Feast of unleavened bread, which was
the day which followed the evening celebration of Passover. If this were
the case then this would mean that Melito was following a synoptic Gospel chronology, which in turn would make Quartodeciman practice
rather inconsistent. However, in Melito's time Jews referred to the Passover rather loosely as the "great feast", and did not make a close distinction between Passover and the following days of unleavened bread. For
this reason too much should not be read into this statement. The festivities which are described are those of the Passover seder, and are by implication the same as those celebrated by Melito. For further details and references see *The Lamb's High Feast*, 148-9.
34 This description of the Jewish celebration is perhaps also as much a picture of the Christian celebration. Note that bread and wine are singled out

81) O lawless Israel, what is this new injustice you have done,
casting strange sufferings on your Lord?
Your master who formed you,
who made you,
who honored you,
who called you Israel.

82) You were not Israel.
You did not see God.[35]
You did not perceive the Lord, Israel,
you did not recognize the first-born of God,
begotten before the morning star,
who adorned the light,
who lit up the day,
who divided the darkness,
who fixed the first boundary,
who hung the earth,
who tamed the abyss,
who stretched out the firmament,
who furnished the world,
who arranged the stars in the heavens,
who lit up the great lights,
who made the angels in heaven,
who there established thrones,
who formed humanity on the earth.

83) It was he who chose you and led you,
from Adam to Noah,
from Noah to Abraham,
from Abraham to Isaac and Jacob and the twelve
patriarchs.

as the foods enjoyed, that the haggadah could be interpreted as the proposal
of a toast, and that dancing was known in the Christian tradition, having particular prominence in *The Acts of John* (so W.C. van Unnik "A note on the
dance of Jesus in the *Acts of John*," *Vigiliae Christianae*, 18 [1964], 1-5).
35 The interpretation of "Israel" to mean "the one who sees God" is found in
Philo, *De mutatione nominum*, 81 and is implied in John 1:45-51.

84) He it was who led you into Egypt,
and guarded you there and sustained you.
He it was who lit up your way with a pillar,
and sheltered you with a cloud.
He cut the Red Sea open, leading you through,
and destroyed the enemy.

85) He it is who gave you manna from heaven,
who gave you drink from a rock,
who gave you the law at Horeb,
who gave you the inheritance in the land,
who sent you the prophets,
who raised up kings for you.

86) He it is who, coming to you,
healed your suffering and raised your dead.[36]
He it is whom you outraged,
he it is whom you blasphemed,
he it is whom you oppressed,
he it is whom you killed,
he it is whom you extorted,
demanding from him two drachmas as the price of his head.

87) Ungrateful Israel, come to trial with me
concerning your ingratitude.
How much did you value being formed by him?
How much did you value the finding of your fathers?
How much did you value the descent into Egypt,
and your refreshment there under Joseph the just?

88) How much did you value the ten plagues?
How much did you value the pillar by night,
and the cloud by day,
and the crossing of the Red Sea?

36 The similarities in the passage just concluded with *Apostolic Constitutions*, 8.12 do not necessitate a common liturgical source, but do indicate that both are drawing on a similar tradition of narrative praise.

How much did you value the heavenly gift of manna,
and the water gushing from rock,
and the giving of the law at Horeb,
and the allotment of the land,
and the gifts given there?

89) How much did you value the suffering ones,
healed by his very presence?
Give me a price on the withered hand,
which he restored to its body.
Give me a price on those blind from birth,
whom he illumined by a voice.
Give me a price on those who lay dead
and who, four days later, were raised from the tomb.

90) His gifts to you are beyond price,
yet you held them worthless when you thanked him,
repaying him with ungrateful acts;
evil for good,
affliction for joy,
and death for life.
On this account you had to die.

91) For if the king of a nation is seized by enemies
a war is fought on his account,
a wall is breached on his account,
a city is ransacked on his account,
ransoms are sent on his account,
envoys are sent off on his account,
so that he might be brought back alive,
or buried if he is dead.

92) But you cast the vote of opposition against your Lord,
whom the gentiles worshipped,
at whom the uncircumcised marveled,
whom foreigners glorified,
over whom even Pilate washed his hands:
for you killed him at the great feast.

93) Therefore the feast of unleavened bread is bitter for
you:
as it is written, "You shall eat unleavened bread with
bitterness."
The nails you sharpened are bitter for you,
the tongue you incited is bitter for you,
the false witnesses you set up are bitter for you,
the ropes you prepared are bitter for you,
the whips which you wove are bitter for you,
the Judas you hired is bitter for you,
the Herod you followed is bitter for you,
the Caiaphas you believed is bitter for you,
the gall you cooked up is bitter for you,
the vinegar you produced is bitter for you,
the thorns which you gathered are bitter for you,
the hands which you made bloody are bitter for you.
You killed the Lord in the middle of Jerusalem.

94) Listen all you families of the nations and see:
a strange murder has occurred in the middle of Jerusalem;
in the city of the law,
in the city of the Hebrews,
in the city of the prophets,
in the city reckoned righteous.
And who has been murdered? Who is the killer?
I am ashamed to say and I am obliged to tell.
For if the murder took place by night,
and if he was slaughtered in a deserted place,
I might have been able to keep silent.
Now in the middle of the street,
and in the middle of the city,
in the middle of the day before the public gaze,
the unjust murder of a just man has taken place.

95) And so he is lifted up on a tall tree,
and a placard is attached to show who has been murdered.
Who is it? To say is hard and not to say yet more fearful.

Listen then, shuddering at him through whom the earth
shook.

96) He who hung the earth is hanging.
He who fixed the heavens in place has been fixed in place.
He who laid the foundations of the universe has been laid
on a tree.
The master has been profaned.
God has been murdered.
The King of Israel has been destroyed by an Israelite right
hand.

97) O mystifying murder! O mystifying injustice!
The master is obscured by his body exposed,
and is not held worthy of a veil to shield him from view.
For this reason the great lights turned away,
and the day was turned to darkness;
to hide the one denuded on the tree,
obscuring not the body of the Lord but human eyes.

98) For when the people did not tremble, the earth shook.
When the people did not fear, the heavens were afraid.
When the people did not rend their garments, the angel
rent his own.
When the people did not lament, the Lord thundered from
heaven,
and the most high gave voice.

99) Therefore, Israel,
you did not shudder at the presence of the Lord;
so you have trembled, embattled by foes.
You did not fear the Lord,
<...>
You did not lament the Lord,
so you lamented your firstborn.
When the Lord was hung up you did not rend your
clothing,
so you tore them over the fallen.

You disowned the Lord,
and so are not owned by him.
You did not receive the Lord,
so you were not pitied by him.
You smashed the Lord to the ground,
you were razed to the ground.
And you lie dead,
while he rose from the dead,
and is raised to the heights of heaven.

100) The Lord clothed himself with humanity,
and with suffering on behalf of the suffering one,
and bound on behalf of the one constrained,
and judged on behalf of the one convicted,
and buried on behalf of the one entombed,
rose from the dead and cried out aloud:

101) "Who takes issue with me? Let him stand before me.
I set free the condemned.
I gave life to the dead.
I raise up the entombed.
Who will contradict me?"

102) "It is I", says the Christ,
"I am he who destroys death,
and triumphs over the enemy,
and crushes Hades,
and binds the strong man,
and bears humanity off to the heavenly heights."
"It is I," says the Christ.

103) "So come all families of people,
adulterated with sin,[37]
and receive forgiveness of sins.
For I am your freedom.
I am the Passover of salvation,

---

37 The word here translated "adulterated" (*pephuromenai*) has oblique reference to the leaven removed from dwellings at Passover.

I am the lamb slaughtered for you,
I am your ransom,
I am your life,
I am your light,
I am your salvation,
I am your resurrection,
I am your King.
I shall raise you up by my right hand,
I will lead you to the heights of heaven,
there shall I show you the everlasting father."[38]

104) He it is who made the heaven and the earth,
and formed humanity in the beginning,
who was proclaimed through the law and the prophets,
who took flesh from a virgin,
who was hung on a tree,
who was buried in earth,
who was raised from the dead,
and ascended to the heights of heaven,
who sits at the right hand of the father,
who has the power to save all things,
through whom the father acted from the beginning and for
ever.

105) This is the alpha and omega,
this is the beginning and the end,
the ineffable beginning and the incomprehensible end.
This is the Christ,
this is the King,
this is Jesus,

38 In this rhetorical climax we may see Melito functioning as a prophet by
speaking the words of the present and risen Christ, speaking to his people
in the assembly, present in his spirit as through the sacramental actions of
the Pascha. The similarities with the "I am" sayings of the fourth Gospel
are striking, and are not fortuitous, for they derive from a common practice of prophecy through the possession of the prophet by the spirit of
Christ.

this is the commander,
this is the Lord,
this is he who rose from the dead,
this is he who sits at the right hand of the father,
he bears the father and is borne by him.
To him be the glory and the might for ever.
Amen.

THE FRAGMENTS AND OTHER MATERIAL

Here may be found a selection of fragments from Melito's work, some testimonies to Melito and a brief selection of other material relevant to Quartodeciman practice. Not all fragments are included, for a full selection may be found in Hall. Those fragments of Melito which are certainly pseudonymous are excluded, as are those which are too small to be useful. Finally a group of fragments, which may belong together and may indeed be parts of another work by Melito, are also excluded. The textual tradition behind these fragments is extremely complex, and we cannot be sure of the exact relationship between them. Given that in themselves they cast little light on *On Pascha* or on the Quartodeciman liturgy, and given the complexity of the tradition, it was felt better to exclude them.

The numbering of the fragments here follows that of S.G. Hall, *Melito of Sardis: On Pascha and Fragments* (Oxford: Clarendon, 1979).

The Fragments

a) Fragment 1 (from Eusebius, Ecclesiastical History, 4.26)

In his book to the Emperor [Marcus Aurelius] he reports that such things were happening against us in his time:

> Now the race of the god-fearing is persecuted, which is something which has never before taken place, afflicted by new decrees in Asia. For the shameless cheats and

those who love the goods of others are, on this pretext, robbing openly by night and by day, seizing the goods of those who have done nothing wrong.

Later on he says:

And if you have commanded that this be done, let it be done aright. For a just king would never desire that wrong be done, and we would count it sweetness to carry off the prize of such a death. This request alone we bring to you: that you should first become personally acquainted with those who cause such discord, and then consider well whether they are deserving of death and punishment, or of prosperity and peace. If this decision and the new decree, a decree unworthy to be used against hostile barbarians, have not come from you, then much more do we beg of you that you should not permit us to endure state-sponsored crime.

Then he goes on saying:

For our philosophy first flourished among the barbarians, blossoming out among your peoples during the illustrious reign of your ancestor Augustus, and became, especially for your Empire, a good and fortunate thing. For from then on the strength of Rome has grown to be great and glorious. To this you have become a much-desired successor and with your son shall continue to be so, guarding the philosophy of the Empire, nursed and originating with Augustus. Your ancestors respected it alongside other cults. That nothing discreditable has befallen the Empire since the reign of Augustus, when the Empire began so auspiciously, and flourished along with our thinking is the best proof of the goodness we intend. But on the contrary, everything has been glorious and splendid, as we all pray that it should. Only Nero and Domitian, persuaded by certain malicious people, were willing to put our activity under attack. It is from them, and through unreasoning custom, that false information about us has arisen like a flood. Your devout ancestors corrected their ignorance, frequently, and in many writings, reprehending those who dared use force against these people. Among them your grandfather, Hadrian, wrote explicitly to Fundanus the proconsular governor of Asia, among many others. Your father, while you were governing alongside him, wrote to the city-governments that no force should be used against us. Among them he wrote to the Larissians and to the Thessalonians and to the Athenians, as to all the Greeks. On your part, since you hold the same opinion concerning these matters, and are greater in your philosophy and philanthropy, we are sure that you will do all that we ask of you.

Comment

The precise context of the new decrees is not known. In this *Apology* (to Marcus Aurelius), Melito is in accordance with the advice laid down by Menander for an address of this kind, in dwelling on the history of the imperial family and in pledging loyalty to the Emperor and to his succession.[1] This is further evidence of Melito's rhetorical education.

b) *Fragment 3 (from Eusebius,* Ecclesiastical History, *4.26)*

In the *Extracts* which he wrote the same author in his preface begins by listing the recognized books of the old covenant. These we must also give here. He writes as follows:

Melito, to his brother Onesimus greetings.

Since you have often asked, in view of your great zeal for the word, that I should make for you extracts from the

1 Robert M. Grant, "Five Apologists and Marcus Aurelius," *Vigiliae Christianae,* 42 (1988), 1-17 at 6-7.

law and the prophets concerning the savior and the whole of our faith, and have further desired to learn the truth about the ancient books, especially with regard to their number and the manner in which they are arranged, I have been keen to do such a thing, knowing your devotion to the faith and love of learning concerning the word and especially given that, as you strive for eternal salvation, you examine these matters more than any others which pertain to God. And so, going to the east, where these matters were spoken and performed, I learned there the books of the old covenant with accuracy. Now I send you my treatise.

These are their names. There are five books of Moses: Genesis Exodus, Numbers, Leviticus, Deuteronomy. Joshua the son of Nave, Judges, Ruth, four books of Kingdoms, two books of Omissions, the Psalms of David, the proverbs and the wisdom of Solomon, Ecclesiastes, the Song of Songs, Job, and among the prophets Isaiah and Jeremiah. There are twelve prophets in one book, and Daniel, Ezekiel and Esdras. From these I have made my extracts, which are divided into six books.

Comment

This fragment is highly significant as the first Christian Old Testament canon. It is also of interest that Melito traveled to Palestine, and is thus an indication that this is the Old Testament canon known by Palestinian Christians, and perhaps Jews. The statement that "these matters were spoken and performed" is interesting since this is a standard definition of a *chreia*, or short aphoristic story, which was a standard element in rhetorical education. The use of this summary of Scripture would imply that Melito understood his extracts from Scripture as a collection of *chreiai*.

c) *Fragment 4 (from Eusebius,* **Ecclesiastical History,** *4.26)*

In his work "Concerning the Pascha" he indicates the time at which he drew it up at the beginning, stating thus:

> When Servillius Paulus was proconsul of Asia, and Sagaris was martyred at a fitting time, there was a great dispute in Laodicea concerning the Pascha, which fell most fittingly in those days. And these things were written:

Clement the Alexandrian records this matter in his own work concerning the Pascha which he says he composed because of Melito's writing.

Comment

For a full discussion of this fragment see the introduction; there it is argued that this is not by Melito at all, but is a scribe's introductory note to Melito's work which Eusebius has copied in error.

d) *Fragment 7 (Anastasius of Sinai,* **The Guide,** *12) (PG 89.197A)*

Of Melito, the bishop of Sardis, from his book on the passion: God has been murdered by an Israelite right hand.

Comment

This fragment, a slight misquotation of *On Pascha* 95, is included since it was the basis on which the original identification of the papyrus was made by Bonner, the first editor of the work.

e) *Fragment 8b (J.B. Pitra,* **Analecta Sacra,** *II 3-5)*

By Melito of Sardis: On Baptism

What kind of gold or silver or bronze or iron is not burned

red hot and then dipped in water, either to be brightened in color or so that it can be tempered through its dipping. Indeed the whole earth is washed with rains and rivers, and farms well after it is bathed. In the same way the land of Egypt is washed by a river in swell, and the cornfield grows and the ear is full, and it yields one hundredfold through the goodly bath. Even the air itself is washed by the raindrops falling. The mother of rains, the multicolored rainbow, itself bathes, when she lures rivers down gullies with watery breath.

If you wish to see the heavenly bodies being dipped go off now to the ocean, and there I shall show you a strange sight. The spread-out sea and the boundless foam and the infinite deep and the measureless ocean and the pure water: the bath-chamber of the sun, the place where the stars are brightened, and the moon's pool. Learn then faithfully from me how they bathe symbolically.

For the sun, when it has run its daily course with its fiery chariot, having in the course of its run become fiery and burning like a lamp, having burned up in the middle of its circular run then, lest he come close by and ignite the earth as though with ten lightning shafts, dips in the ocean. In the same way a sphere of bronze, full of interior fire, and shedding much light, is dipped in cold water with a loud noise and leaves off burning. But the fire within is not extinguished but returns once more when it is roused. In the same way then the sun, having flamed like lightning, is bathed in cold water but does not cease to burn entirely, for its fire is unsleeping. When he has washed in this symbolic bath he rejoices greatly, having water for food. He is one and the same sun, although he appears to people as new; he has been tempered in the deep and purified in a bath. He has driven the darkness of night away and begets a bright day. Along his course operate the movement of the stars and the appearance of the moon. For they bathe in the bath-chamber of the sun as faithful disciples. For the stars and the moon together follow the trail of the son, permeated by his pure brilliance.

If the sun, together with the stars and the moon, is bathed in the ocean, why should Christ not bathe in the Jordan, the King of the heavens and the ruler of creation, the sun of uprising who appeared to mortals in Hades and on earth alike, and who rose alone as a sun out of heaven?

Comment

Remarkable parallels between this fragment on baptism and stoic exegesis of Homer have been noted.[2] The first section, concerning the uses of water, contains images generally found in stoic treatments of the doctrine of providence. Stoics had a particular interest in the interpretation of poetry and so the technical background to Melito's study here is almost certainly Homeric exegesis. This is exactly what one would expect from the author of *On Pascha,* where there is a section which engages with the question of exegetical method in a stoic manner. As part of his rhetorical training Melito would have learnt the schools of Homeric interpretation. The authenticity of this fragment has been doubted, but there are grounds for seeing it as authentic, quite apart from the fact that the author of this fragment shared an educational background with Melito. The main reason for suggesting inauthenticity is stylistic but the difference in style between this fragment (reminiscent in many ways of a school exercise) and *On Pascha* may be accounted for by recognizing the difference in genre. *On Pascha* is liturgical, this fragment is controversial.

---

2 By Robert M. Grant, "Melito of Sardis on Baptism," *Vigiliae Christianae,* 4 (1950), 33-36.

f) Fragments 9-11 (from a catena published by J.B. Pitra, Spicilegium Solesmense, II lxiii s)

Fragment 9

Of blessed Melito of Sardis.

As a ram he was bound,
he says concerning our Lord Jesus Christ,
and as a lamb he was shorn,
and as a sheep he was led to slaughter,
and as a lamb he was crucified.
And he bore the wood on his shoulders,
going up to slaughter like Isaac at the hand of his father.
But Christ suffered.
Isaac did not suffer,
for he was a type of the passion of Christ which was to come.
Yet even the type caused fear and astonishment to come
upon people.
For it was a strange mystery to behold:
the son led up a mountain by his father, for slaughter,
whose feet he bound onto the wood of the offering,
preparing with haste for the slaughter to come.
Isaac was silent whilst bound like a ram,
not opening his mouth nor uttering a word.
He did not fear the knife,
nor did he panic at the fire,
nor did he grieve at his suffering.
The type of the Lord he bore bravely.
In the midst was Isaac offered,
like a ram bound at his feet.
And Abraham was present and held the knife unsheathed,
not ashamed to put his son to death.

Fragment 10

Of Melito of Sardis

On behalf of Isaac, the righteous one, there appeared a

ram for slaughter
so that Isaac could be set free from his bonds.
The ram was slaughtered and ransomed Isaac:
in the same way the Lord was slaughtered and saved us,
and freed us from our bonds,
and ransomed us through his sacrifice.

Fragment 11

A little later:

For the Lord was a lamb like the ram which Abraham saw
caught in a Sabek tree.
But the tree displayed the cross,
and that place showed forth Jerusalem,
and the lamb showed forth the Lord, tied up for
slaughter.

Comment

The chief interest in these fragments, all of which come
from the same collection of testimonies, is Melito's use of tra-
ditions deriving from Judaism concerning the redemptive effect of the sacrifice of Isaac and his concern to counter them.
Melito refers to this theme in *On Pascha,* 59 and 69, where
Isaac is a type of Jesus. We may perhaps see some hint of Isaac
typology in John's Gospel, in which Jesus, like Isaac, carries
the wood (the cross) for his own sacrifice, and we should also
observe that there are a number of references to Isaac's sacrifice in *The Martyrdom of Polycarp.* Melito is concerned to
stress that Jesus is greater than Isaac in that he is actually sacrificed and dies.[3]

---

3 For further discussion see Robert L. Wilken, "Melito, the Jewish Community at Sardis and the Sacrifice of Isaac," *Theological Studies,* 37
(1976), 53-69.

g) *Fragment 17* (Bodmer papyrus *XII*)

> You saints sing hymns to the father,
> you maidens sing to the mother.
> We hymn them, we saints lift them high.
> You have been exalted to be brides and bridegrooms,
> for you have found your bridegroom Christ.
> Drink wine, brides and bridegrooms...

Comment

This fragment is found in papyrus Bodmer 12, following on from *On Pascha*.[4] It is not actually attributed to Melito, but Perler suggests that it is part of the Quartodeciman liturgy, and that it is the beginning of the second book mentioned by Eusebius.[5] It is quite possible that it is a fragment of the liturgy, and that this is the reason for its inclusion in the manuscript. But this does not mean it is necessarily the work of Melito, nor is there any certainty whether this is part of the other book, assuming that such a book ever existed. Perler suggested that the liturgy was baptismal, and followed on from the invitation to forgiveness at the end of *On Pascha*. But not only is there no definite reference to baptism in *On Pascha*, the function of *On Pascha* as a liturgy of commemoration rather precludes a further baptismal rite. The forgiveness, or rather the recognition of forgiveness, is more likely to be experienced in an additional cup, analogous to that added onto the Jewish seder. If that is the case then this liturgical fragment could well be part of the liturgical (and paraliturgical!) rite of drinking and rejoicing which might follow on from Melito's revelation of the exalted Messiah at the conclusion of the formal haggadah.

4 See the introduction, p. 10.
5 Othmar Perler, *Ein Hymnus zur Ostervigil von Meliton? (Papyrus Bodmer 12)* (Freiburg: Paradosis 15, 1960).

Testimonies to Melito from later authors

a) *From Eusebius* (Ecclesiastical History, *4.26*)

At this time both Melito, the bishop of the community in Sardis, and Apollinarius of that in Hierapolis were flourishing and prominent. Each individually addressed an apology in these times to the emperor of Rome mentioned above, in defense of the faith. Treatises have come down by these people to our knowledge: of Melito, two books on the Pascha, *On conduct and the prophets*, that *Concerning the church*, and the work *Concerning the Lord's day*. Then there is that *Concerning human faith*, and that *On the creation* and that *On the obedience of faith and on sense*, and additionally that *Concerning the soul and the body and their union*, and that *On baptism* and that *On the truth* and *On the foundation and the birth of Christ*. And his work *On prophecy*, and that *Concerning hospitality* and *The key*. And that *Concerning the devil and the Apocalypse of John*, and that *On the embodiment of God* and last of all the short book to Antoninus.

Comment

The remainder of Eusebius' testimony is made up of the three extracts from Melito's work found above numbered as 1, 3 and 4 (of which 4 is not actually by Melito!) The text of Eusebius' list here is impossibly corrupt, and the division of the words into titles, and in some cases the words themselves, is little more than intelligent guesswork. The probability is that Eusebius had done little more than consult a library catalogue, or perhaps more than one catalogue, and for this reason we should not be overmuch exercised by the reference to "two books on the Pascha."[6]

6   There is a good discussion of this list, including reference to the textual problems, in Hall, *Melito of Sardis: On Pascha*, xiii-xvii.

b) *From Jerome,* **On Famous Men,** *24*

Melito the Asian, the bishop of Sardis, gave a book to the Emperor Marcus Antoninus Verus, who was a disciple of the orator Fronto, on behalf of the Christian faith. He wrote other books, and these are some which we catalogue here: Two books *On the Pascha*, one book *On the life of prophets*, one book *On the church*, one book *On the Lord's day*, one book *On the senses*, one book *Concerning faith*, one book *On creation*, one book *On the soul and the body*, one book *Concerning baptism*, one book *On the truth*, one book *On the generation of Christ*, one book *Concerning his prophecy*, one book *On hospitality* and another book which is called *The key*. One book *On the devil*, one book *On the Apocalypse of John*, one book *On the embodiment of God* and six books of *Extracts*. In the seven books which he wrote against the church on behalf of Montanus, Tertullian complains at his elegant and declamatory genius, and adds that he is considered by some of us to be a prophet.

Comment

The list of works is clearly based on that of Eusebius and has no independent value. The snippet on Tertullian's cavil however is interesting. For Tertullian to complain at another's declamatory style is extraordinary, though the substance of his report of Melito's style is borne out in *On Pascha*. The report of Melito's prophecy bears out the reading of the final sections of *On Pascha* as ecstatic prophecy spoken in the name of Christ. The interesting question is, who considered Melito a prophet? Although Jerome would be indicating that the catholic side (of the catholic-Montanist debate) recognized Melito's prophecy, the use of "us" in Tertullian usually indicates that he is referring to the pro-Montanist sub-group within the church at Carthage, and is possible that Jerome has been careless in his citation, and that Tertullian, who does not reckon Melito a prophet, is angered at his fellow-Montanist sympathizers who nonetheless recognize Melito's prophecy. Certainly there is every indication here that Melito was considered a prophet by his contemporaries, and that this provides grounds for us to understand his work in this light.

Selections from other authors concerning Quartodeciman practice

a) *Apollinarius (from the* Paschal Chronicle, *PG 92.80-81)*

Apollinarius, the most holy bishop of Hierapolis in Asia, who was roughly contemporary with the apostles, taught similarly in his treatise on the Pascha, saying as follows:

> Now there are some who through ignorance love to quarrel about these matters: but what they maintain in this affair is forgivable. For ignorance does not respond well to accusations, but may be amenable to teaching. And they say that on the fourteenth day the Lord ate the sheep with the disciples, and that on the great day of unleavened bread he suffered, and they say that Matthew speaks thus, according to their interpretation. But their thinking is not in accordance with the law, and the Gospels conspire to refute them.

In the same work the same writer speaks thus:

> The fourteenth is the true Pascha of the Lord,
> the great sacrifice,
> the son of God standing in place of the lamb.
> The one being bound is the one who bound the strong man,
> and the one being judged is the judge of the living and the dead.
> And the one who is betrayed into the hands of sinners to

be crucified is raised above the horns of the unicorn.
And the one whose holy side was pierced
poured forth from his side the two purifications:
water and blood,
word and spirit.
He is buried on the day of Pascha,
and a stone is put over his tomb.

Comment

The second of these two fragments is a classic statement of
Quartodeciman theology: there is no doubt that Apollinarius
was a Quartodeciman, despite some avowals to the contrary.
He also wrote against Montanism, and is clearly a rough contemporary of Melito. The dispute which is mentioned here is a
matter of much debate; I have argued elsewhere that there was
some debate among Quartodecimans about the time of the paschal celebration (though there was agreement on the date.)
Some kept it in the evening, and justified their practice with
reference to synoptic accounts of Jesus eating the Passover
with his disciples, whereas others (Apollinarius and, probably,
Melito among them) kept it at midnight and justified their
practice with reference to John. Both justifications are secondary. Those who kept Pascha in the evening understood it to be
a repetition of the Last Supper, whereas those who kept at
night reckoned it a commemoration of the passion and resurrection, as is implied by Melito's work.[7]

b) Hippolytus

(from the Paschal Chronicle, PG 92.80-81)

Hippolytus now, a martyr of sanctity, who was the Bishop

---

7 For full bibliography and discussion see Alistair Stewart-Sykes, *The
   Lamb's High Feast* (Leiden: Brill, 1998), 147-60, though note the caveat
   below in footnote 8.

of Porto near Rome, writes in this way in his anthology against all the heresies:

> I see now what the cause of the disquiet is. For somebody might say "Christ kept the Pascha and then, during the day, he died. It is necessary for me to do what the Lord did, just as he did it." They are in error in not realizing that Christ suffered (*epaschen*) at this hour, and did not eat (*ephagen*) the Pascha according to the law. Thus he was himself the Pascha which was announced in advance, and which was fulfilled on the appointed day.

(from the Refutation of all the Heresies, *8.18)*

There are others, fractious by nature, individualistic in their understanding, pugnacious over the point, who maintain that it is necessary to keep the Pascha on the fourteenth of the first month in accordance with the provision of the law, on whatever day it might fall. They have regard only to that which is written in the law that whosoever does not keep it as it is commanded is accursed. They do not notice that the law was laid down for the Jews, who in time would destroy the true Passover, which has come to the gentiles and is discerned by faith, and not by observation of the letter. By keeping to this one commandment they do not notice what was said by the apostle, namely "I bear witness to everyone who is circumcised that they are obliged to keep the entirety of the law." In other things they conform to everything which has been handed down to the church by the apostles.

Comment

Hippolytus is widely assumed to be writing in these passages against Quartodeciman practice.[8] It is however possible

8 An erroneous assumption which I made myself in *The Lamb's High Feast*, 157-58. I withdraw my criticism on this point of G. Visonà,

that he was himself of Asian or Syrian lineage, which means that he might himself be a Quartodeciman. If this could be imagined for a moment we might see that rather than writing against Quartodecimans he is defending the practice of keeping Pascha at midnight rather than in the evening at the same time as the Jewish festivity, using a similar line of argument to Apollinarius. On this understanding his opponent is a Quartodeciman who believes that the synoptic chronology and the law alike point in the direction of keeping Pascha as the fulfillment of the Last Supper; Hippolytus replies by suggesting that the true fulfillment of the Pascha is not the Last Supper but the manner in which the Lord fulfilled and completed the provisions of the law by suffering (*paschein*) rather than eating (*phagein*). The manner in which both Hippolytus and Apollinarius refer to the fractious and difficult nature of their opponents is also an indication that the dispute is not between Sunday-keepers and Quartodecimans but between Quartodecimans with different understandings of the time at which to keep the Pascha, and thus of what it means to keep the Pascha.

c) Eusebius' account of the Quartodeciman controversy at Rome at the end of the second century (Ecclesiastical History, 5.23-24)

23) Now there was stirred up at that time a dispute of no small moment, for all the residents of Asia, for whom this was an ancient tradition, held it necessary to keep the feast of the Pascha of the Savior on the fourteenth day of the moon, when the Jews are commanded to sacrifice the sheep. They held it required at all costs to put an end to their fasting on that day, regardless of what day of the week it was. This was not in accordance with the custom and manner of all the churches in the

"Pasqua Quartodecimana e cronologia evangelica della passione," *Ephemerides Liturgicae,* 102 (1988), 259-315.

rest of the world, who, according to apostolic tradition maintained the custom which had come to them that they should not conclude the fast except on the day of the resurrection of our Savior. Synods and gatherings of bishops were convened on this matter and all with one mind drew up the church's opinion for universal dissemination. They decreed that the mystery should not be celebrated except on the Sunday on which the Lord rose from the dead, and that on that day alone should the paschal fast be concluded. The writing which came from those who were gathered in Palestine, who were brought together under Theophilus, bishop of the community of Caesarea and Narcissus, of the community in Jerusalem, is extant to this day. The same is true of another communication from Rome concerning the same dispute, which shows that Victor was the bishop. There is another from the bishops in Pontus, over whom Palmas, as the oldest, presided, and from the communities of Gaul which Irenaeus governed. And there is yet another from Osrhoene, and the cities there. And similarly from Bacchyllus, the bishop of the church of the Corinthians, and a host of others, who expressed one and the same opinion, and gave the same judgement. And so there was one decree, as we have shown.

Comment

Victor was simply a bishop among others, in what was still a loose confederation of churches. The episcopal office in Rome grew out of the office of the presbyter whose duty it was to correspond with other churches; it is still in this capacity that Victor is corresponding with other churches in the world over a matter which concerned Rome, and it is from this that Eusebius deduces that he was the sole bishop. It would seem that Asian churches in Rome were continuing their Quartodeciman practice, and that this was an obstacle in the gradual unification of the Roman churches under a single acknowledged bishop; quite why Victor is addressing himself to communities outside of Rome over a purely internal matter is not clear, but it is possible that Asian (and other Quartodeciman) communities in Rome had appealed to their home bishops, and so Victor is attempting to set the record straight.

24) Polycrates was the leader of the bishops of Asia, who firmly maintained that they should keep the custom which had been handed down to them from ancient times. And he himself sets down the tradition as it had come down to him in the following letter which he wrote to Victor and to the church of the Romans.

> For we keep the day without interference, neither adding nor subtracting. And there are in Asia great lights who have died, and will rise again on the day of the coming of the Lord, when he comes with glory from the heavens and shall raise all the saints: Philip of the twelve apostles, who lies in Hierapolis, and two of his daughters who grew old in virginity. And there is another daughter of his who rests, having served the church in the Holy Spirit. And there is indeed John who lay on the breast of the Lord, who was a priest wearing the breastplate, and who was a martyr and a teacher.[9] He lies at Ephesus. And indeed there is Polycarp in Smyrna, both bishop and martyr, and Thraseas from Eumeneia, who lies at Smyrna. And is it necessary to speak of Sagaris, bishop and martyr, who lies at Laodicea? And there is Papirius the blessed, and Melito the eunuch, who governed all things in the Holy Spirit, and who lies at Sardis awaiting the visitation from the heavens when he shall be raised

9 For an extensive discussion of this puzzling reference see Richard Bauckham, "Papias and Polycrates on the origin of the Fourth Gospel," *Journal of Theological Studies,* ns 44 (1993), 24-69.

from the dead. All of these kept the fourteenth day as the Pascha in accordance with the Gospel, not deviating from the rule of faith but maintaining it. And then there is myself, Polycrates, the least of all; I have kept to the tradition of my race, some of whom I have followed. For seven of my race were bishops, and I am the eighth.[10] And my race always kept the day when the people put away the leaven. I therefore, brothers, sixty five years in the Lord and having had commerce with brothers from the whole world and having spanned the whole of holy scripture, am not frightened by threats. For those better than I have said: we should obey God rather than people.[11]

To these remarks he adds comment concerning the many bishops who were present with him and agreed with him.

I might record the bishops who are with me, whom I invited when you desired that I should invite them. If I should write their names they would be a great multitude. They see me, the least of men, and they have approved this letter, knowing that I do not have gray hair for nothing but that I have conducted myself always in the Lord Jesus.

At this, Victor, presiding over Rome sought to cut off straightaway the churches of all of the community of Asia from the common union, together with those which neighbored upon them, on the grounds of heterodoxy. He denounced them in letters proclaiming that the brethren there

10 See the introduction, p. 3, for some discussion of what Polycrates means by his reference to his race. Although Polycrates considers himself a minor figure in comparison to his predecessors, he is clearly the acknowledged leader of the Asian bishops, though whether this results from family connections, wealth, age or the occupation of the see held by John cannot be said.

11 Acts 5:29. Polycrates is quoting Peter!

were entirely out of union. But this was not to the liking of all
the overseers, and they pleaded with him to have a mind to
those things which are conducive to peace and to unity with
one's neighbors and to common charity. These letters are extant, criticizing Victor severely. Among them was Irenaeus,
who wrote in his capacity as leader of the brethren in Gaul, in
which he states that one should keep the day of the resurrection
of the Lord on the Lord's day alone. Yet he takes Victor to task
for cutting of entire churches on the grounds that they kept an
ancient custom which had been handed down to them, and he
gives much counsel besides, adding, in these words:

> For the controversy is not only about the day, but also
> concerning the very form of the fast. For there are those
> who hold that one should fast a single day, others two,
> and others more. Some count "the day" as forty continu-
> ous hours of day and night. And the great variety of ob-
> servance did not come about in our day, but came from
> much earlier, from those who went before us, who held
> closely to their customary ways, perhaps in their sim-
> plicity, and so things have been done until our time. But
> nonetheless all of these were at peace, and we likewise
> live in peace with one another. Indeed, the distinction in
> fasting emphasizes the harmony of our faith.

To these remarks he adds the following account, which I
may suitably quote, since this is its proper place:

> Among them were the elders before Soter, who presided
> over the church which you now lead. We mean Anicetus
> and Pius, Hyginus and Telesphorus and Sixtus. None of
> them observed, nor did any of those who were with them.
> And yet those who did not observe kept peace with those
> from the communities in which the observance was kept,
> and they engaged with one another. And the custom of
> observance was all the more difficult to those who did

not observe at all. And never was anyone cast out over this affair, but those elders before you who did not observe nonetheless sent the eucharist to those from the communities who observed. And when the blessed Polycarp was at Rome in the time of Anicetus, although there were many other matters on which they had differences, they maintained peace with one another, not wanting to fall out with one another over this matter. Anicetus was not able to persuade Polycarp not to observe, as he had with John the disciple of our Lord and the other disciples with whom he had associated, and as he had always observed. Nor moreover did Polycarp persuade Anicetus to observe, for he said that he should be faithful to the custom of the elders before him. And although matters stood thus, nonetheless Anicetus yielded presidency of the eucharist to Polycarp in the church, clearly out of respect for him. And they parted from one another in peace, as indeed the entire church had peace between those who observed and those who did not observe.

Comment

Although Eusebius does not understand the material with which he is dealing, since he clearly treats Victor not only as a monarch-bishop in Rome but as a bishop having authority even beyond the city, the phrases which he uses are possibly derived from ancient documents. Victor is not excommunicating Polycrates, but Asian churches within Rome, and the common union from which they are expelled is the union of churches within Rome. Irenaeus' mention of the sending of the eucharist would seem to be a reference to the ancient Roman rite of the *fermentum,* in which churches in the city would send portions of the eucharist to the other churches in the city as a sign of their union. It is this sign of union which is withdrawn and which, according to Irenaeus, should be sent even though there is some difference among the Roman churches. Irenaeus was himself Asian in origin, though would seem not to keeping Quartodeciman practice in Gaul, and he points out that there are differences even among the Quartodecimans with regard to the length of the fast which is kept before Pascha.

The references to "observing" however in Irenaeus' letter are matters of great controversy, as the verb has no object.

An implied object might be:

The fast, by which Irenaeus means that some did not observe an extended fast before Pascha

The feast, by which Irenaeus means that some did not observe a Pascha at all, or

The fourteenth day, which would imply that some at Rome observed Pascha on a Sunday, others on the fourteenth day.

All of these are historically possible (though grammatically the second suggestion is difficult and the first is easiest, especially since Irenaeus in the previous passage has used the same verb to refer to the fast.) However, not observing the fast might be an implication that the feast was not observed either: the eventual compromise to which the Tiburtine tables point, that the Pascha was set on the Sunday following the 14th Nisan and that the fast would begin on the 14th, would be a reasonable compromise between those who observed no fast or annual festival and held that Sunday was the only proper day for the (weekly) commemoration of the resurrection and those who observed Pascha on the 14th Nisan. This still leaves us blind to the majority Roman practice between Soter and Victor however.[12] Victor is moving the Roman church towards monepiscopacy, and

12 It is possible that an annual festival was kept on a Sunday, though without a prior fast.

therefore desires some measure of liturgical uniformity in any event, but the problem would be all the more acute should the fast fall on a Sunday and therefore displace the usual Sunday celebration. This is why Irenaeus points out that those who did not observe nonetheless sent the eucharist to the non-observers, that is to say that, although the Quartodecimans might be observing no celebration on a particular Sunday, the non-Quartodeciman Roman Christians nonetheless sent them a portion of the eucharist. Thus the solution proposed here is that on grammatical grounds we should read "fast" as the object of "observe," but that the effect of this was that those who observed no fast observed no feast either.[13]

d) From the Life of Polycarp, 1 (Ed. J.B. Lightfoot, The Apostolic Fathers, II.3; repr.; Peabody MA: Hendrickson, 1989), 432-465

In the days of unleavened bread, Paul, coming down from Galatia, came into Asia, intending from there to go on to Jerusalem. He thought it to be a great rest to be among the faithful in Smyrna after his immense labor in the Lord Jesus Christ. In Smyrna he came upon Strateas, who had heard him in Pamphylia, and was the son of Eunike, the daughter of Lois. They are mentioned in his writing to Timothy, when he speaks of "the unfeigned faith which is in you, as it dwelt first in your grandmother Lois and in your mother Eunike." From this we may deduce that Strateas was Timothy's brother. When he arrived Paul gathered those who were faithful and spoke to them about the Pascha and the Pentecost, reminding them of the new covenant of the offering of the bread and the cup, how they should be sure always to celebrate it in the days of unleavened bread, holding fast to the new mystery of the passion and the resurrection. Here the

---

13 For a fuller discussion and bibliography see *The Lamb's High Feast,* 205.

apostle is clearly teaching us that we should not do this outside
of the period of the unleavened bread, as the heretics, and especially the Phrygians do, but nor should we be obliged to
keep the fourteenth day, for nowhere is the fourteenth mentioned, but he mentions the day of unleavened bread, the Pascha and the Pentecost, in keeping with the Gospel.

Comment

This text probably derives from a period immediately after
the Council of Nicaea, at which point Quartodecimans disap-
pear from the catholic church. The statement here prefaces a life
of Polycarp, perhaps with the intention of repudiating any
Quartodeciman claim in Smyrna on the basis of Polycarp's
practice. The Phrygians, to whom reference is made here, are
Montanists. This group was found mainly in rural Asia. They
were Quartodeciman, in common with all other Asian Christians, but it appeared that due to isolation they were unable to
compute the time of Pascha, and so kept a solar Pascha, that is to
say that they kept Pascha on a fixed date in a solar calendar,
rather than the lunar calendar employed in Judaism. This would
lead them to keep Pascha often outside the time of unleavened
bread, namely the week following Pascha. Epiphanius,
Panarion, 50.1 also records Quartodecimans in Asia who keep
a solar Pascha. His account is very confused, but the confusions
which had come about among the Quartodecimans at his time
could be explained due to the use of a solar calendar among iso-
lated groups. It is significant that Epiphanius traces the origin of
Quartodeciman practice to Montanism, an indication that the
only Quartodecimans known in his day were Montanist.

e) A selection from the Syrian Didascalia, 21

For this reason, from the tenth, the second day of the week, you shall fast for the Pascha. You will be sustained by bread and salt and water only at the ninth hour until the fifth day of the week. On Friday however and the Sabbath fast completely, and do not taste anything. Gathering together at night keep vigil and watch the whole night in prayer, watching and reading the prophets and the Gospels, and with psalms, with fear and trembling and with diligent intercession until the third hour of the night which is after the Sabbath. Then finish your fast. For we also fasted in this way when the Lord suffered, bearing witness to the three days, and we were keeping vigil and praying and watching for the annihilation of the people, because they erred and did not know our redeemer. Thus also you should pray, that the Lord should not hold their guilt against them to the end, that they may not be condemned as they condemned the Lord, but that they should be given room for repentance, conversion and pardon for their iniquity. Pilate, the judge, was a heathen and a stranger, yet he did not consent to their wicked deeds, rather he took water and he washed his hands and he said, "I am innocent of the blood of this man." The people then answered and said "His blood be on us and on our children." And Herod ordered that he be crucified, and Our Lord suffered on our account on the Friday. Therefore you should especially keep the fast of the Friday and the Sabbath, and also keep vigil and watch on the Sabbath, reading the Scriptures and the Psalms, praying and interceding for those that have sinned, in confident expectation of the resurrection of the Lord Jesus, until the third hour of the night which is after the Sabbath. Then offer up your offerings, and from then on eat and rejoice, and sing merrily. For the earnest of our resurrection, that is Christ, has risen. And this shall be an ordinance to you for ever, until the end of the ages.

Whenever the fourteenth of the Pascha occurs, keep it then. For the month and the day do not fall at the same time every year, because it is variable. Therefore when the people is keeping the Pascha you should be fasting, and take care to perform your vigil within their [?feast of] unleavened [bread].

Comment

The Syrian *Didascalia* gives instructions for the Pascha. In its present redaction it is not Quartodeciman, but there are clear signs that a document of Quartodeciman provenance has been included and worked over in the course of compiling the *Didascalia*. Indications of Quartodeciman practice can be found in the anti-Judaism of the outlook of the vigil and in the concern that the Pascha be fixed in accordance with the Jewish Pesah. The pattern of vigil with prayer and fasting and with reading of Scripture, followed by joyful feasting and singing, is exactly that to which Melito bears witness. *On Pascha* provides for a homiletic reflection on Scripture, followed by a hymnic celebration of Christ's resurrection triumph to accompany the feast. So this document gives us an idea not only of the liturgical context in which we can read *On Pascha*, but also of the mood which would attend the celebration to which *On Pascha* points us.

f) *From Theodoret's* Compendium of Heretical Tales, *3.4 (PG 83.405)*

The Quartodeciman heresy has this supposition: they say that the evangelist John preached in Asia and taught them to celebrate the feast of the Pascha on the fourteenth day of the moon. They have a defective understanding of the apostolic tradition for they do not wait for the day of the Lord's resurrection but might keep the third day, or the fifth, or the Sabbath, or whatever day it might occur, and celebrate with praise the memory of the passion. Moreover they employ falsified acts of apostles and other falsehoods far removed from grace, which they call "apocrypha."

Comment

Although roughly contemporary with Epiphanius, Theodoret is clearly far better informed. It is possible that Quartodeciman practice had lived on in his area of Syria. In particular we should note the manner in which the Quartodecimans claim a Johannine tradition and a lunar Pascha, which is consonant with Melito's Christian tradition, the statement that the means of celebration is praise (actually he says "panegyric," which is good description of *On Pascha* as rhetoric), the statement that the center of the feast is commemoration, and finally that the content of commemoration is actually the passion as much as the resurrection. The reference to falsified acts could well involve reference to the *Gospel of Peter*, with which Melito was certainly familiar and which seems to derive from a Quartodeciman milieu, since it presupposes a Johannine passion chronology and states that the apostles kept a fast whilst awaiting the resurrection.

g) *Epistula Apostolorum 15*[14]

After I return to my Father you are to remember my death whenever Pascha comes about. Then will one of you be thrown into prison on account of my name, and will be in trouble and sorrow because he is in prison while you are keeping Pascha, and he is not keeping the festivity. For I shall send my power in the form of my angel and the gates of the prison shall be opened. He will come out and will watch with you and remain until the cock crows, when you will have completed my agape and my commemoration, and he will be thrown once again into prison as witness to me, until he comes out and

---

14 *Epistula Apostolorum* is extant in two different versions, one Ethiopic, the other Coptic. What follows is a somewhat conjectural reconstruction of the original Greek eclectically based on both versions.

proclaims as I have commanded. So we said to him: "Lord, have you not fulfilled the Pascha? Is it necessary that we should take the cup and drink it again?" He replied "It is indeed necessary, until I return with those who died for me."

Comment

The points of interest in this text (which do not depend on conjectural reconstruction) are:

a) That the festival is kept in memory of the passion

b) That a vigil forms part of the celebration

c) That it is a night festival, complete by dawn

d) That there is a commemorative meal-rite.

The significance of all of this in the reconstruction of the Quartodeciman celebration should be very clear.

The first part of the apostles' question, concerning the Lord's fulfillment of the Pascha, is not found in the Coptic version. However it seems to reflect the same concerns about whether the feast is to be timed according to the Jewish celebration or after that are reflected in the citations of Hippolytus and Apollinarius above.

Bibliography

This short bibliography is restricted to works in English. Other works are cited in the footnotes, and further bibliography can be found in *The Lamb's High Feast*.

Two key works head the list, notably:

S.G. Hall, ed. and trans., *Melito of Sardis: On Pascha and Fragments* (Oxford: Clarendon, 1979).

This provides a critical text, an accurate translation on facing pages, some useful notes and a valuable introduction.

A. Stewart-Sykes, *The Lamb's High Feast: Melito, Peri Pascha and the Quartodeciman Paschal Liturgy at Sardis* (Leiden: Brill, 1998).

The only full-length work on Melito and on the Quartodecimans in English. Much of the content of this introduction and the notes on the translation presuppose the technical discussions in this work.

Jewish and Christian Paschal liturgies

Gordon J. Bahr, "The Seder of Passover and the Eucharistic Words," *Novum Testamentum,* 12 (1970), 181-202.

A good introduction to the outline of the Jewish rite on which that of Melito was based.

Baruch M. Bokser, *The Origins of the Seder: The Passover Rite and Early Rabbinic Judaism* (Berkeley: University of California, 1984).

A very thorough treatment of many of the issues surrounding the reconstruction of early Jewish Passover rites.

Deborah Bleicher Carmichael, "David Daube on the Eucharist and the Passover Seder," *Journal for the Study of the New Testament,* 42 (1991), 45-67.

Reviews the contribution of Daube, to whom much of the reconstruction offered here is indebted, especially in his two works listed below.

David Daube, *He That Cometh* (London: Diocese of London, 1966).

David Daube, *Wine in the Bible* (London: Diocese of London, 1974).

S.G. Hall, "Melito in the Light of the Passover Haggadah," *Journal of Theological Studies,* ns 22 (1971), 29-46.

A vital contribution to the study of Melito, identifying the literary form of *On Pascha* as that of a paschal haggadah.

J. Jeremias, *The Eucharistic Words of Jesus* (ETr) (London: SCM, 1966).

A classic, though probably wrong on every count!

G.A.M. Rouwhorst, "The Quartodeciman Passover and the Jewish Pesach," *Questions Liturgiques,* 77 (1996), 152-73.

A good brief treatment of the subject.

S. Stein, "The Influence of Symposia Literature on the Literary Form of the Pesah Haggadah," *Journal of Jewish Studies,* 8 (1957), 13-44.

An interesting work, noting the manner in which the Passover celebrations of the Jews are at home in the Hellenistic world.

Étienne Trocmé, *The Passion as Liturgy* (ETr) (London: SCM, 1983).

An interesting work which, though not on Melito, sees the liturgical aspect of the Passion narrative.

Solomon Zeitlin, "The Liturgy of the First Night of Passover" *Jewish Quarterly Review,* ns 38 (1947-1948), 431-460.

Sardis

G.M.A. Hanfmann, Fikret Yegül, and John S. Crawford, "The Roman and Late Antique Period," in *Sardis from Prehistoric to Roman Times: Results of the Archaeological Exploration of Sardis 1958-1975,* Ed. G.M.A. Hanfmann (Cambridge MA: Harvard UP, 1983), 139-67.

G.M.A. Hanfmann and Hans Buchwald, "Christianity: Churches and Cemeteries," *Sardis from Prehistoric to Roman Times: Results of the Archaeological Exploration of Sardis 1958-1975,* Ed. G.M.A. Hanfmann (Cambridge MA: Harvard UP, 1983) 191-210.

D.G. Mitten, "A New Look at Ancient Sardis," *Biblical Archaeologist,* 29 (1966), 38-68,

A very accessible treatment of the archaeological evidence.

A.R. Seager, "The Building History of the Sardis Synagogue," *American Journal of Archaeology,* 76 (1972), 425-35.

Began the task of challenging the role of the synagogue in understanding Melito's attitude towards Judaism.

Paul Trebilco, *Jewish Communities in Asia Minor* (Cambridge: Cambridge University Press, 1991).

Has a chapter on Sardis.

Melito as rhetorician

A. Manis, "Melito of Sardis: Hermeneutic and Context," *Greek Orthodox Theological Review,* 32 (1987), 387-401.

A good attempt to see the scriptural interpretation of Melito in context, though marred through a misdating of the synagogue (for which he is not uniquely guilty!) and by a failure to recognize that historical typology is not the opposite of allegory (for which he is likewise not uniquely guilty!).

Thomas Halton, "Stylistic Device in Melito *Peri Pascha*," in *Kyriakon: Festschrift Johannes Quasten*, ed. Patrick Granfield and Josef A. Jungmann (Münster: Aschendorff, 1970), 249-55.

A. Wifstrand, "The Homily of Melito on the Passion," *Vigiliae Christianae*, 2 (1948), 201-23.

The first to observe the relationship between Melito's style and that of contemporary rhetoricians.

Melito and later hymnody

B.G. Tsakonas, "The Usage of the Scriptures in the Homily of Melito of Sardis On the Passion," *Theologia*, 38 (1967), 609-20.

E.J. Wellesz, "Melito's Homily on the Passion: an Investigation into the Sources of Byzantine Hymnography," *Journal of Theological Studies*, 44 (1943), 41-8.

Melito's anti-Judaism

A. Stewart-Sykes, "Melito's Anti-Judaism," *Journal of Early Christian Studies*, 5 (1997), 271-83.

S.G. Wilson, "Passover, Easter and anti-Judaism: Melito of Sardis and Others," in *To See Ourselves as Others See Us: Christians, Jews, "Others" in Late Antiquity*, Ed. Jacob Neusner and Ernest S. Frerichs (Chico: Scholars, 1985), 337-56.

Technical historical issues (mentioned but glossed over in the introduction

W.H. Cadman, "The Christian Pascha and the Day of the Crucifixion: Nisan 14 or 15," *Studia Patristica*, 5 (TU 80; Berlin: Akademie, 1962), 8-16.

C. Dugmore, "A Note on the Quartodecimans," *Studia Patristica*, 4 (TU 79; Berlin, Akademie, 1961), 411-21.

S.G. Hall, "The Origins of Easter," *Studia Patristica,* 15 (TU 128; Berlin, Akademie, 1984), 554-67.

Cyril C. Richardson, "The Quartodecimans and the Synoptic Chronology," *Harvard Theological Review,* 33 (1940), 177-90.

Cyril C. Richardson, "A New Solution to the Quartodeciman Riddle," *Journal of Theological Studies,* ns 24 (1973), 74-84.

It is an indication of the difficulty of this subject that the second article by Richardson is a recantation of the first!

Other literature

Richard Bauckham, "Papias and Polycrates on the origin of the Fourth Gospel," *Journal of Theological Studies*, ns 44 (1993), 24-69.

The best treatment of Polycrates' letter to Victor, demonstrating the Johannine roots of Quartodeciman practice, and much else besides.

Campbell Bonner, *The Homily on the Passion by Melito Bishop of Sardis and some fragments of the Apocryphal Ezekiel* (London: Christophers, 1940).

The first edition of *On Pascha.*

P. Kahle, "Was Melito's Homily on the Passion Originally Written in Syriac?" *Journal of Theological Studies,* 44 (1943), 52-6.

The answer is: of course not, but the Syriac fragments are interesting in their own right, as they show the extent to which it was easy for Melito's work to find a home in Quartodeciman and anti-Jewish Syria.

T.J. Talley, *The Origins of the Liturgical Year* (Collegeville: Liturgical, 1986).

A valuable work by a historian of patristic liturgy who once taught at the General Theological Seminary in New York which contains discussion of the Pascha and of Melito.

Index

ST VLADIMIR'S SEMINARY PRESS
1-800-204-2665 • www.svspress.com